ICE
Fishing

Jerry Chiappetta

ICE
Fishing

STACKPOLE BOOKS

ISBN 0-8117-2041-1
Library of Congress catalog card number: 66-22828
A revised edition of *Modern ABC's of Ice Fishing*

Printed in the U.S.A.

acknowledgments

Any work like this requires a lot of assistance from
different people with different talents and information.

The author would like to thank the representatives
from the various fish and conservation agencies in the
United States and Canada, and those many people from
companies manufacturing ice fishing equipment for their
help. Special thanks should go to Dick Lehman of the
Michigan Conservation Department, Gene Little, Art
Best, The Arnold Tackle Company, Jim Crowe, Gordon
Charles, and the editors of The Stackpole Company for
their patient guidance.

J. C.

Dedicated to my wife, Pat,
who puts up with all my fishing
and the time I spend writing about it.

contents

chapter 5
baits for fish, large and small

chubs and shiners 77/hooking a minnow 81/worms 83/ insect baits (dragonflies, mayflies, stoneflies, caddis flies, hellgrammites, wood borers, goldenrod gall, mighty mousies, mealworms and corn borers) 85/other natural baits 92

chapter 6
ice flies and lures

secrets of an expert 98/color, flash, and movement 99/fly fishing in winter? 101/plastic lures 104

chapter 7
how to catch panfish

the sunfish family 108/putting the bait to work 111/perch 113/rigs for perch 116/crappies 117/smelt 118

chapter 8
fishing the big ones

lake trout 122/eating habits of fish 123/Northern pike 125/mr. muskellunge 127/chain pickerel 128/walleye 131/sauger 132/whitefish 133

chapter 9
spearing through the ice

the sportsmanship of spear fishing 136/decoys 137/spearing techniques 139/the importance of dark and quiet 141/ novelty spearing 142/the sturgeon 143

chapter 10
conservation and sportsmanship

greater productivity of ice fishing 147/the ice fisherman's necessary function in conservation 152

chapter 11
ice fishing in different regions

the United States 155/Canada 173

Reader's Guide to
Ice Fishing in Different Regions

THE UNITED STATES

CANADA

introduction

The ice fisherman of yesteryear used to be a heavily plumaged bird whose call was "Eee-ee-egads-my-toes-are-froze." He was wrapped in so much wool he looked like a clothes rack from a second-hand store as he waddled across a crust of thin blue ice barely strong enough to support a tubercular kiwi bird.

He was like the creature George Mead wrote about in his diary, "Fishing in Lake Simcoe," on March 6, 1815 in Ontario, Canada. Mead wrote that while skating on the big lake "there was what appeared to be a mound of earth. As I approached, I thought I perceived it move a little. I stood for some seconds wondering what I should do, and had almost determined to go home for my gun when I saw the hide which caused all my speculation thrown suddenly aside to make way for the head and shoulders of an Indian. He had so completely enveloped himself in a large buffalo skin that no part of his head, body, hands or feet were to be discovered. He sat over a square hole cut in the ice, with a short spear

9

ready to transfix any fish which might be attracted to his bait . . . an artificial fish of white wood with leaden eyes and tin fins . . ."

In Canada or the United States, early ice fishermen were a strange breed, often accused of being a little "teeched" in the head to find some sort of pleasure in subjecting themselves to the rigors of winter. Like the fishermen Mr. Mead wrote about, other early North American winter anglers were masters at improvising. They had no "store-bought" fishing gear. They had to make their own. They had no printed information about ice fishing, because they were such a scattered, tight-lipped, independent group that secrets—and even the most basic techniques—were not openly discussed, let alone written down for mass consumption.

In the thumb area of lower Michigan, they still tell the story of the Russian immigrants who brought the fabulous Russian spoons and Russian hooks to the United States. When a stranger approached one of these successful fishermen who brought their know-how from the Old World, the Russian would cut his horsehair line and let the lure sink to the bottom rather than permit any "outsider" to find out what kind of fish attractor he had down there. They also used to hide their catch in the snow. When you asked the age-old question, "Howyadoing?", the secretive Russian would grunt something under his big fur collar and not even look you in the eye. Any attempt at further "conversation" only brought a deeper chill.

The art of winter fishing, for generations, was something held close to the hearts of relatively few rugged outdoorsmen who could be identified, in season, by their red, wet noses, frozen, jigging fingers, and one pant leg frozen from stepping into old fishing holes. Their common expression was a scowl each time the sun shone bright and the weather turned warm. At home this crafty cuss would never stir from his fireplace to walk to the corner drug store unless he had two hot bricks in his pockets. But when the ice was on the pond and the wind howled out of the north, something within him stirred and out he went to sit on his favorite lake.

Today, the modern ice fisherman still has that restless stir, but he is a different individual. For one thing, he doesn't have to be a masochist, since new developments in outdoor clothing have taken the suffering out of the sport. There are insulated rubber boots so warm that their wearers perspire in them if they are not careful. There are one-piece subzero suits which are relatively inexpensive, lightweight, comfortable, and even colorful and stylish. Many manufacturers now produce all the equipment the winter angler needs, and competition has kept the prices within reason and the quality of these goods fairly high.

No longer does the ice fisherman have to walk long distances from the end of the plowed road to a wilderness lake or river. The modern ice fisherman rides a snow-sled. If the fish are not biting, the ride itself through the quiet winter wonderland is worth the trip. These same snowmobiles and tremendous improvements in winter clothing have lured added thousands of the very young and very old into the ranks of the more than six million ice fishermen.

Our aim in *Modern ABC's of Ice Fishing* has been to assemble for the first time all the modern methods of angling through a hole in the ice from all across North America and as far south as Arizona, a place we normally think of as desert and burning sun. The ice fishing zone of this continent covers almost everthing north of a line from the Atlantic through New Jersey westward through Missouri and Kansas, then south to Arizona and northwest again through Oregon. It has been made legal in California. In a survey of more than thirty states with ice fishing, we found that Michigan was the nation's leader with approximately half a million winter anglers. Minnesota, equally blessed with thousands of lakes which freeze solid from around December through March and early April, was next in line, with an estimated 422,000 ice fishermen as of 1965, according to the Sport Fishing Institute. In these two midwest states alone, ice fishermen plunked down more than 15 million dollars in 1965 for licenses, baits, equipment, and special clothing. It is anyone's guess how much the winter anglers of North America spend each winter.

Our study showed that the most desirable and most prized winter fish caught, by a margin of more than two to one, was some species of trout. Perch were next in preference followed, in this order, by bluegills, walleyes, Northern pike, pickerel, crappies, smelt, and whitefish. You'll meet these fish and many more that are important to winter fishermen in the pages which follow. Also we tried to give a regional rundown, by states, on where anglers do their fishing, how they do it in different areas, and when. Because licenses and seasons tend to change from year to year, we have not attempted to give all the dates and seasons for every state, but we do report on the general regulations for the important ice fishing states.

We can comment here that some states must hire college-trained specialists for writing confusing and contradictory fishing regulations. This is changing, however, and more and more states are trying to take the needless restrictions out of their fish laws and instead of making you feel like an intruder, they are holding out a welcoming hand to ice fishermen.

Nebraska is a good example of one of the more progressive states. The motto in "Nebraskaland" is "we attempt to make catching fish just as easy and as much fun as possible and avoid imposing a lot of unnecessary rules." Of all the states and provinces, the Yukon gives the best bargain for a $2 non-resident fishing license. As of 1965, fishermen were allowed, each day, twenty Arctic grayling, five lake trout or Dolly Varden trout, five kokanee salmon, five rainbow or cutthroat trout, two steelhead, two king, chinook, or coho salmon, and only twenty Northern pike. What about that for a bargain?

Certainly modern ice fishing has come of age. It has come out from behind that high fur collar and it now smiles a cheery welcome to all today. Ice fishing and ice fishermen have changed. "At the present rate of increase in the sport," a Minnesota Conservation Department biologist said, "it is believed that many of these lakes may soon provide more recreational hours to the winter ice fisherman than they do to the summer angler."

It is for these ice fishermen that this book was written. *Modern ABC's of Ice Fishing* begins where all other fishing books end—with winter.

J. C.

one

the well-dressed ice fisherman

Late in the fall as the ducks and geese wing south, the hunter hangs up his gun and the fair weather fisherman stores his gear for the long winter ahead. This is the time of year when the ice fisherman stirs with excitement all across North America.

A friend of mine once told me, "Ice fishing would be great and I'd try it, but I get cold. And when I'm cold, I can't have fun."

He is right. Anyone who is frozen and miserable can't

possibly be enjoying himself. But today, the modern ice fisherman doesn't have to suffer any longer. New clothes have taken the shiver out of winter.

the body's defenses against cold

To better understand how humans adapt to cold, let's examine the body's natural defenses, which are really amazing. A "thermostat" in the brain turns down the flow of blood to the skin surface and the extremities in order to protect the vital organs. Your nose and mucous membranes warm the frigid air in the few inches between the nose and the lungs so the body can tolerate the air. The skin also reacts to cold by forming "goose bumps" and begins shivering. These goose bumps, anthropologists claim, are a hangover from caveman days when humans were supposed to have worn a natural fur coat. The bumps would ruffle up that fur to better insulate against the cold. Shivering is actually an exercise for the skin, which isn't getting its normal shot of warming blood.

This is the body's calculated risk—to sacrifice the ears, nose, fingers, and toes to preserve the more important parts such as the brain and heart. This same thermostat also causes the heart to speed up, increasing the body heat inside so that it actually produces an interior fever.

According to research at the University of Rochester, doctors found as much as a forty degree difference in the warmth of the body areas. All this is not a completely involuntary action. The U.S. Army has also done research in subzero cold and found that if they gave the volunteer subjects a thirty-second warning that a certain finger was going to be dipped into ice water, the blood flow to the skin of that finger dropped off before the finger was actually dunked!

The Army also confirmed that shivering is a form of skin exercise which the average person can keep up for hours. Then the muscles become tired and lose their ability to shiver. That's a danger sign. Lack of shivering leaves the victim prey to the cold.

Stooping or hunching over is another involuntary action the body makes in the cold. This is just another way of protecting those inner organs. Persons in the last stages of "freezing to death" are always in a balled-up position with arms and legs rigidly pulled in tight. Even when a cold victim reaches this state of affairs, all is not lost. There have been scores of accounts of people found "frozen stiff" who survived with no ill effects.

One Milwaukee woman survived after having a body temperature of more than twenty-seven degrees below normal. A Woonsocket, R.I., man recovered without ill effects when he was found with a body temperature of only sixty degrees. When a person gets this cold, doctors report, the blood turns to sludge. This is what causes death, they say. Red cells of the blood lose their ability to carry oxygen, and the freezing person really suffocates to death.

the head

The most important single piece of clothing for the ice fisherman is his head covering. The head is one part of the body which continues to get its steady, even supply of warm blood. This makes it the most vulnerable spot. Next to going without a good cap and/or hood, drinking alcoholic beverages outdoors to "fight the cold" is the worst thing you can do. Alcohol gives an artificial, temporary warmup, followed by a severe letdown in the body's ability to really stay warm. Drinking gives this false feeling of warmth by causing blood to flow to the skin surface, exactly where it shouldn't go.

Good headgear is a heavy wool cap with a peak and ear flaps. You won't win any style shows, but the flaps will protect the back of your head, ears, and part of your neck. A cap with a peak will also give some protection from the glare of the snow and ice, a topic which will be discussed later. On extremely cold days, a long coat or a one-piece overall outfit should have a hood to pull up over the cap.

Select a good hood with a strap or drawstring so it can be pulled in snug. No clothing yet designed will generate heat. Well-made outdoor clothes, however, will be made so they do the best job of preventing the escape of body heat. And as this heat will rise within your clothing, critical spots to check heat escape are around the neck and head.

the body

For generations, all outdoorsmen felt the only respectable material to be worn against the wind and cold was wool. There was good reason for feeling this way. Wool is good, because it has many trapped air spaces in the fibers to act as insulation. But wool also has some serious drawbacks. Invariably, it needs professional dry cleaning. Wool is subject to constant insect attacks and requires special protection and storage in the off season. It shrinks and wears out in cleaning and hard use. And there is nothing wetter than wet wool, as any veteran outdoorsman knows.

Wool itself will not cut the wind, the biggest bugaboo. To beat the wind, ice fishermen must burden themselves with many layers of wool and then top that off with a windbreaker of plastic or rubberized material. Multi-layers of heavy wool restrict a fisherman's movements, and he looks like Mr. Five-By-Five struggling out on the ice.

In the 1950s, the popularity of waterfowl down insulation material rose. Down-filled underwear, down-filled pants and coats, and even down-filled socks and mittens were the rage and, in some areas, still are today. The trouble with down is the cost.

Down is very light. It does dry fast and is reasonably easy to compress for storage and packing. It can be laundered as well as dry cleaned and it isn't as susceptible to insect predation as wool. It is fair in wind also. If you can afford down-filled pants and coats, great.

The U.S. Air Force has developed a down-filled Arctic survival suit which protects a man at 50° below zero. This is a hooded coat extending to the feet with a drawstring which converts it into a sleeping bag. It also has snaps to form legs, allowing the wearer to walk in the outfit. Down-filled boots with leather soles and matching mittens with a windbreak parka complete this outfit. It can be squeezed down into a container the size of a shoe box, and it weighs around seven pounds.

The Air Force also gave us the World War II leather flight suit with sheepskin lining, a common ice fishing outfit still around today. It is hard to beat leather as a windbreaker. The trouble with this outfit is the weight and its year-to-year keeping qualities. Leather is very heavy and stiff in the cold. It dries and cracks easily without special care.

After considering all the factors—weight, water-repellent ability, warmth, flexibility, price, storage and bulk —the nearly perfect ice fishing, subzero outfit is the new one-piece insulated coverall. Best coverall suits have a great hood which is form-fitting to come around and down to your eyebrows and close around your cheeks. These suits also have tight-knit nylon cuffs and zippers from the crotch to the chin and down the insides of the legs from knees to ankles. One of these coveralls I use has 100 per cent nylon shell and lining and is filled with polyester. It's a good idea to buy these extra large. You can dress in street clothes, with a light pair of cotton-wool combination underwear, and then slip into the coveralls once you arrive at the fishing spot. The extra large, heavy-duty zippers allow you to pull the suit on over your boots without struggling.

With such an outfit, it is not necessary to put on several heavy shirts and extra heavy underwear. And by opening or closing the large zippers at the neck, you can control the heat inside the outfit while walking or chopping holes in the ice.

the feet

More complaints are heard about cold feet than anything else. There is no simple answer because different pairs of feet can tolerate different amounts of cold. There are two rules which apply to all feet: do not wrap them up so tightly they get no circulation, and do not allow them to perspire, because they will soon get cold.

We recommend one pair of heavy socks made of a

Well-dressed ice fishermen (*Courtesy Michigan Department of Conservation*)

combination of wool and man-made fibers, such as olefin, rayon, and stretch nylon, and a little cotton. They provide good insulation inside a pair of rubber thermo boots to keep feet dry and comfortable.

Some ice fishermen don't need this same footwear combination to be comfortable. They get along well with two heavy pairs of wool socks or one pair of cotton and one pair of heavy wool socks. Over these they wear extra large sheepskin-lined bedroom slippers and old-fashioned four-buckle Arctics.

Another combination is felt packs or boot liners, the same packs deer hunters have used for many years, worn inside high rubber boots. Always wear rubber in ice fishing because of the water and slush usually encountered on the ice. The water comes up when a new hole is cut or when the warm sun melts some of the snow on the more solid ice.

Prevent perspiration when walking or working on the ice by loosening the strings or unbuckling your boots. This allows fresh air to circulate and some of the heat to escape from around your feet. Another good reason for keeping boots loose is so that you can kick them off should you be unfortunate enough to break through the ice. Water-filled boots act like two anchors when a man is fighting to keep afloat. (See the chapter "safety on the ice" for information on rescuing yourself and others.)

the hands

An ice fisherman's hands, in and out of the water and in and out of the minnow bucket, are always a problem if he is not prepared with knowledge and the right equipment.

First, always take two pairs of gloves. Three are even better. One pair will always manage to be wet. The ideal setup is two pairs of wool gloves and one pair of heavy mittens.

Big mittens should be pinned or clipped to a string or elastic band which crosses your shoulders and the back of your neck so that when you are working the mittens will hang out of the way. This cord or band will also keep them from falling into the water and slush.

It is a good idea to wear a pair of 20¢ cotton gloves while cleaning fish out on the ice. They afford some protection from the sharp fins and help in holding the fish while gutting them out, something you should do whenever slackening action allows a spare moment. By the way, once the fish are cleaned, do not allow them to become frozen solid on the ice. Thawing them at home for more careful cleaning and scaling or skinning and then refreezing them is not a good practice. They can be kept cold, but not frozen, by packing them in the snow or putting them near your lantern or inside your fishing shelter.*

Once you are finished handling the fish, these cheap gloves can be used in holding a delicate minnow for re-baiting a tipup. Fishermen tend to squeeze the life out of a minnow with cold, numb fingers because the minnow is wet, slippery, and hard to hold without gloves. Hang these work gloves next to your lantern or heater, where they have a chance to dry out.

---

*For detailed information on how to clean fish and keep them from spoiling, see *New Fisherman's Encyclopedia,* Ira N. Gabrielson, ed., $19.95; and Bradford Angier's *Wilderness Cookery,* $3.95 (Pap.), both published by The Stackpole Co., Cameron & Kelker Sts., Harrisburg, Pa.

the face

We already mentioned the snug hood and cap with the peak or visor, but a smart ice fisherman will also pack sunglasses or ski goggles in his tackle box or sled. Goggles give you protection from sudden wind and snow storms as well as some help from the bright glare.

Face masks such as those one-piece, knitted affairs worn by some skiers are very comfortable on blustery days, too. Be sure to buy one with a long neck for added warmth.

All the clothing and wearing apparel thus far described should be considered minimum for the well-dressed ice fisherman. Most of the time, such a well-dressed fisherman needs only his fishing tackle, heater or lantern, lunch, thermos of hot coffee, tea, or soup, spud or auger, minnow bucket and fishing license to have a grand day on the ice.

The very latest 1975-style ice fishing clothing not only includes all of the previously mentioned features of warmth, light weight, etc., but also is capable of keeping a man afloat in the water.

Clothing manufacturers originally designed such flotation coveralls for oil workers who had to operate in cold weather on off-shore rigs. And within the past few years, all of our "well dressed" ice fishermen have adopted these flotation outfits. Prices for such suits normally are over $100.00.

two

A Spartan ice fisherman needs nothing more than the clothes on his back and his hook, line, and lure or bait, but it is far more fun and a great deal more comfortable with some sort of shelter and some accessories. The list of "necessary" items can grow to such a point you'll need a tractor to haul all the junk onto the ice. Naturally, to be within the practical limits, it's best to keep it down to a load easily towed on a sled or loaded into a snowmobile.

A few years ago all the rods, reels, and necessary tackle

the winter angler needed were either homemade or snitched from the summer tackle box. Today, there is no need to put fancy and expensive fair-weather rods and reels through the punishment of winter fishing. Today there are special, yet inexpensive, ice fishing rods and reels for every kind of fishing, from the dainty nibbling panfish to the mighty lake trout. Reels in shallow water, ten feet or less, are not really necessary, though many anglers like the convenience of a reel. For many, a reel, then, is an accessory. Some fishermen really cut the gear to the bone. Hook and line is all you need, they say.

the rod

A novice at ice fishing always asks, "What sort of rod?" And he's shocked when the oldtimers say, "None." A rod, like a reel, is a luxury for most. They use them only for small fish.

Fishermen who continue to try to use a standard spinning or casting rod while still fishing through a hole in the ice are handicapping themselves. The long rods designed for flinging a plug force ice fishermen to stand five feet or more back from the hole. When they break down a two- or three-piece rod and use just the butt section, they have a stiff pole which will cause them to miss the bites of the sneaky bait snatchers like perch and bluegills. A fair substitute panfish rod is a delicate tip section from an old fly rod, but an improvised reel holder is required with such an outfit. Most of the "store-bought" tipups are so much better than anything that can be built in the basement, it doesn't pay to waste time trying to make your own.

the tipup

This is not an accessory; this is a must. Tipups started out as a couple of sticks across the ice hole with a third stick on a pin or nail which stuck down into the water. At the end of this middle or third stick of wood is an underwater reel which does not freeze up as long as it is beneath the surface, naturally. Some old-style tipups, also called "traps" in parts of the ice fishing country, had the reels above water. They worked until they got wet; then they froze tight.

The line coming off the reel causes the reel to turn when the fish takes the bait. The reel, in turn, triggers a stiff wire or narrow strip of metal which flips up and waves its tiny flag. The fisherman, usually watching his tipups from a cozy shanty or shelter nearby, then swings into action.

There are many variations of this setup. Recently out are new-style metal tipups made of aluminum tubing, but the method of operation is about the same: The rig is lowered into the hole, the line and bait are dropped down, the line is set on the trigger, and when a bite comes, the flag goes up. One outfit has a battery in it and when the fish pulls, the red flashing light goes on. This is fine for night fishing (where it is legal) or for fishing in a fog or when it is snowing.

The tipup, regardless of its make or style, is a prime tool for the ice fisherman, and it is used for everything from jumbo-size perch all the way up to the mighty muskellunge. One angler I know, John Ezdebski of Ludington, Michigan, took a monster sturgeon on a tipup while fishing for pike in February, 1965.

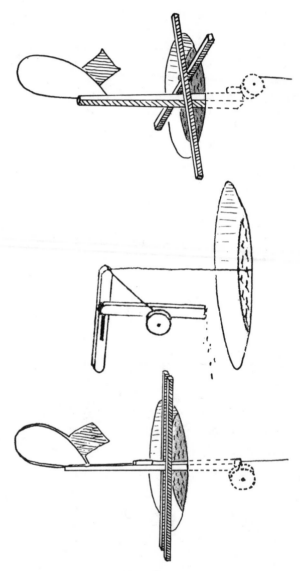

Three types of tipups (Courtesy New York Department of Conservation)

New-style tipup with underwater reel and an auger for quickly and easily cutting a hole *(Courtesy Michigan Tourist Council)*

John Ezdebski of Ludington, Michigan, with his 101-pound sturgeon, probably the largest fish ever caught on a tipup. He was fishing for Northern pike with 15-pound test line. *(Photo by John Ezdebski)*

He was fishing on Pere Marquette Lake with a large minnow on a fifteen-pound test line on a tipup. Around 2 P.M. on that dreary, overcast day, the flag on John's tipup began to wave frantically. He ran to the tipup and watched the underwater reel spin as the big fish stripped off line.

"A real big baby," he said to himself. "Maybe a fifteen-pounder?"

Taking the tipup and reel in hand, he played the fish for forty-five minutes, giving a little line, picking up a little, but always cautious not to try to hold when the big fish wanted to run. Finally, he got the fish up near the hole and was amazed to see that he had tied into a sturgeon, a very rare creature to catch on a hook and line in summer or winter.

John called for help from two friends who brought gaff hooks and worked to enlarge the hole. Eventually they straightened out both gaffs, pulling the monster sturgeon through.

It weighed 101 pounds and was six feet long, unofficially the largest fish caught in modern times on a tipup with fifteen-pound test line.

Ezdebski admitted his record catch was an accident, that he was originally fishing for pike. His thrill of a lifetime was comparable to that of a bluegill fisherman who suddenly has hold of a big bass or muskie on light tackle.

equipment to wear

Most fishermen can get along well most of the time with good rubber boots. Most frozen lakes will have enough snow over the ice to provide walking traction, but on some occasions metal ice cleats are needed. These strap around the boot, fitting up under the arch so they bite into the ice. They give cat-claw gripping and are important for older folks who have reached an age where a sudden spill onto solid ice would mean a serious fracture.

Another handy item to wear is a compass. I say "wear," because the best compass is one being used, and the pin-on compass is small and out of the way pinned to the left side of a windbreaker. No need to remove your gloves and fish down through several layers of clothing to get out a compass when it is pinned there, always ready to serve you.

Fishermen who use very large inland lakes or frozen bays in the Great Lakes should always have a compass. It may seem unimaginable that one could get lost on a lake while ice fishing, but once you get caught in a blizzard or in the dark when you stay out later than you had planned to, you'll never be without a compass a second time.

Carrying a compass is one thing. Knowing how to use it is another. In a nutshell, the simplest method is to take a reading from your starting point and then reverse your course to get back. Pick a prominent landmark, church tower, or other high point. In night fishing, take a sighting off a light that will remain on during the night.

In total darkness or a "white out" caused by a blizzard, remember your walking time in any one direction. If it took you thirty minutes to walk out from your car or from the landing, keep this in mind when heading back. Allow yourself a few extra minutes. You should—after reading this book—be loaded down with fish and weary from carrying them off the ice.

The compass is also a tool which, when used in connection with bottom maps, helps you find weed beds, dropoffs, and reefs where the fishing usually is better.

equipment to carry

The list could be endless here, ranging from carrying your lunch to carrying the latest stock market report to read while waiting for the fish to bite. But there are two standout items for carrying, especially when walking out and back from the fishing area. These are a long-handled spud and about fifty feet of strong, lightweight nylon rope.

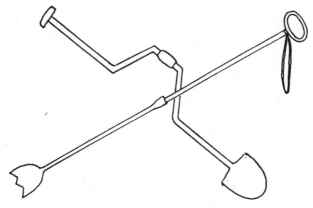

Ice spud and shovel-type auger (*Courtesy New York Department of Conservation*)

If you are breaking a new trail on the ice, then it is doubly important to have that spud in hand and that rope slung over your shoulder. The spud is for tapping and probing the ice ahead of you, and the rope is to throw to a partner or a passerby should someone break through. More on saving yourself or someone else in the chapter, "safety on the ice."

To start your fishing, that spud or ice chisel will serve

the purpose of punching out a hole in the ice, but it will frighten away fish by its banging on the ice. It is wise to spud several holes at once but in different areas, so you can move to the spare holes, knock out the thin crust of new ice which will form, and begin fishing immediately.

An easier way is to use one of the many ice drills or augers available at any sporting goods or well-stocked hardware store. Even easier yet is to use one of the gasoline-powered augers. The auger has been a boon to ice fishermen, cutting down the work of creating a new fishing hole and encouraging fishermen to move more often, and in doing so to find more fish.

An axe makes a sloppy hole. If the ice is thin enough to be hacked through with an axe, it's too thin to be really safe. Four inches is the minimum safe thickness. An axe might be useful if you are on a wilderness lake where there is some firewood nearby for a cooking or warming fire. But since too many of us are forced to use crowded lakes with cottages lining the shores, plan on carrying your own fuel, such as kerosene, gasoline, or charcoal for heating and cooking.

This leads to another accessory—a small stove. Some feel this is going beyond the reasonable limit, but for many fishermen or a man and his family, it is a very necessary item. There's nothing like freshly brewed hot chocolate to keep mom and the kids interested. And you'd be amazed how much helpful information strangers on the ice will volunteer about what bait is taking the fish. This information, of course, flows faster when the stranger is drinking your steaming coffee or chocolate. You could say it's a good way to break the ice with your fish-catchin' neighbors.

This fisherman can drill a hole very easily with this screw-type drill. *(Courtesy Michigan Tourist Council)*

In my outdoor travels, I have picked up a very handy one-burner gasoline stove which breaks down and folds up into a compact package about six inches by six inches square and about three inches thick. It is a self-generating dandy which runs forever on a cup of regular automobile gasoline. Once filled, the heat of your hands causes expansion inside the small chamber and soon a fine spray of misty gas spurts through a pinhole in the coils. Presto—you're cooking with gas. The little burner costs around $7, and I have been using mine for five years for ice fishing and big game hunting.

Another ultralight heater is the handwarmer which, when you can get it working properly, slips neatly into a pocket. It's not a bad idea to carry several, one in your coat and a couple in your pants pockets.

Lanterns give both light and heat. It is very common to see a lone ice fisherman sitting on a small ice sled with a lantern down between his legs and a blanket draped over his shoulders to keep out the wind and keep in the heat.

All these items—the handwarmers, small cook stoves, and lanterns—should be filled and tested before going out on the ice. Out there in the cold is no place to start tearing one of these gadgets down to try to get them operating.

cameras

Fish caught through the ice are usually cooked, eaten, and forgotten unless you hang up a record-size buster on the fireplace mantel, but photographs of your fish and your trip afford pleasure year after year. Taking pictures out on the ice requires a little caution.

Going from a warm car or cottage to the frigid air won't harm a camera, but returning from the cold to a warm area will fog lenses and cause condensation inside the equipment. Avoid the extremes. The cold will make your film stiff, and an attempt to advance it rapidly might cause it to rip. Carry your camera next to your body, beneath your coat. If you want to be sure your camera won't freeze up, have it winterized. This means the factory has to remove all lubrication, a move more necessary with motion picture cameras than with still cameras.

Very cold movie cameras tend to slow down, resulting in overexposure and/or "Keystone Cops" movement of characters when the film is shown. Remembering to keep all cameras warm, but not too hot, will avoid 90 per cent of the trouble.

A waterproof Army surplus ammunition box is ideal for carrying cameras, film, and extra lenses on the ice. Pad the sides, bottom, and lid with sponge plastic or sponge rubber to give the equipment protection from bumps and some insulation against the weather. Another tip: Remember that the ice and snow reflect light from the bottom up. Be careful to take light meter readings up close to your subject, in order to avoid glare, which gives a false reading. This is true with black and white or color film. Automatic or magic-eye cameras can't think for themselves, regardless of what their manufacturers say in their ads. Again, move in close, so the stray light and glare don't confuse your built-in light meter or magic-eye camera. When changing film, go inside a shanty or shelter or cover your camera with a cloth to keep out all that stray light which might fog the film.

Once the used film is out of the camera, place it inside

A new boat-sled is fine for fishermen who can afford it. The cost of this unit was just under $5,000. (Courtesy Aquanautics, Inc., Mountain View, California)

one of your pockets close to your body to warm it gradually. Taking it directly into a warm, humid cottage or car might cause damage to the latent image. And then, once it is warmed up, have it processed as soon as you get back home for the very best results, especially with color film.

mechanized transportation

Snowmobiles and air sleds which glide over ice and snow have opened up countless back country lakes to the ice fisherman and now permit the very young and very old to enjoy this winter sport. Now there is an unusual boat-sled which uses an airplane pusher type propeller. The boat-sled is at home on ice and snow or in open water, making it a fine craft for ice fishermen, who never again have to worry about the thickness of the ice. There are two drawbacks. It is not large enough to carry much gear, and it costs around $4,800.

Snowmobiles which start at around $750 and go up to several thousands of dollars, all work about the same. They have gasoline engines from six horsepower and up which drive a rubber tractorlike belt. This continuous-drive belt digs into the snow and ice and pushes the craft, which is steered by a pair of short skis in front. Some snowmobiles have enough power to scoot along at speeds up to forty-five miles per hour in snow and even faster on clear ice, but on clear ice they are not very controllable.

The primary advantage of a snowmobile, of course, is that it permits moving around easily if fishing is slow on your side of the lake, and you can go cross country to reach lakes which get very little fishing pressure.

A word on courtesy. Snowmobiles do rumble. Any noise

Lightweight, canvas, pop-up shelters (*Courtesy Michigan Department of Conservation*)

like that sets up vibrations which do not help the fishing. Make a wide sweep around other fishermen and never go so fast that you lose control.

shelters

Old-style ice shanties or dark houses which look like rural outhouses are being replaced at many ice fishing communities by the lightweight, canvas, pop-up shelters which double in the summer as camping outfits.

Windbreaker (*Courtesy New York Department of Conservation*)

They are not usually as warm and windproof as the sturdier wood and tarpaper shacks, but the super-duper ice shanty isn't necessary anymore with modern clothing. The simplest form of shelter is the plywood or canvas windbreaker or lean-to. Another of these is the familiar

Indian tepee setup. Material stretched between two up-right poles is one windbreaker. Round poles about six feet long and 1½ inches in circumference are needed. Canvas or some other strong material like heavy plastic is tacked to them. At each end of the poles are spike nails which are driven into the ice to hold everything down. Snow and slush ice are piled around the bottom to keep the wind from getting under.

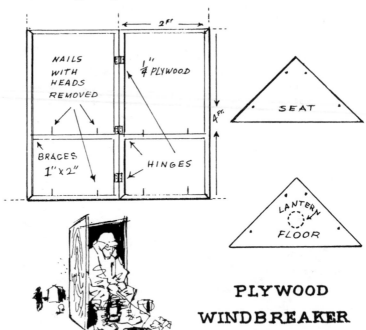

Plywood windbreaker (*Courtesy Michigan Department of Conservation*)

Another simple, portable windbreaker is made from a pair of two four-foot sheets of quarter-inch plywood. These are hinged. This all folds up and, by putting run-

ners on one side, you can use it as a sled. Slightly below
the middle and at the bottom of the plywood sheets, horizontal braces are put in place, each with four nails which
are driven in vertically. The nails are deheaded so they
will slip through positioned holes in two triangular boards
which serve as a portable seat and floor. When this windbreaker is not being used, the seat and floor are stored
inside the two folded sheets.

Slightly up the luxury and cost ladder are the two-man
pop-up tents which open like an umbrella and those
canvas shelters which stretch over a pipe framework. The
frame of such a rig is usually held to a wooden sled floor
with runners. You fish through a hole in the wooden floor.
Most of these already have a hole in the top or side with
a fireproof insulation material where you vent your stove.
Summer tents like this have to have a slight alteration
to accommodate the stovepipe outlet.

By far, the two shelters just described are the most
popular because they are a happy combination of economy, comfort, and portability. These units all fold neatly
for off-season storage. They are also compact enough to be
carried in the trunk of a car or in the back of a station
wagon. They are also high enough so you can stretch your
legs and roomy enough for two men, a small stove, and
their gear.

In New England and Canada there are community-type
fish houses, which are like long hallways set over a trench,
with a dozen or more anglers manning lines fastened to
bicycle wheels on axles pinned to the wall over the opening.

A lot more specialized and elaborate is the dark house
shanty for the spear fisherman seeking sturgeon, muskies,

pike, and other large fish. The spearing shanty or dark house resembles a rural outhouse from the outside. It is almost always a one-man building with a six- or seven-foot ceiling to accommodate the long-handled spear. The big difference between the spearing house and other shelter is that this one has to be light-tight like a photographer's darkroom.

Ice shanties *(Courtesy New York Department of Conservation)*

The floor has to have a large rectangular opening, roughly two by three or two by four feet for spearing and getting the fish through. In a sturgeon-spearing shanty, of course, everything is larger. While an average Northern pike might be two or two and a half to four feet long, some sturgeons are more than six feet long. Make sure the door of the spearing shanty is large enough and easy enough to open so that you can back out of it while wrestling your speared fish out of the water. Otherwise, heavy wooden shanties, which also can be rented on many

Ice shanty town on Michigan's Houghton Lake *(Courtesy Michigan De-partment of Conservation)*

popular lakes, can be as elaborate or as simple as your personal tastes. Some have shelves, carpeting, enough food for a winter vacation stay, and even portable television. Where the ice freezes early and stays late, some shanties in Canada and along the U.S.-Canadian border even have electric power lines installed. At Tip-Up-Town*, U.S.A., during the ice fishing festival on Michigan's Houghton Lake, the telephone company puts out a public pay telephone booth on the ice.

odds and ends

There is no end to the list of odds and ends an ice fisherman might want to take with him. While the most important items have already been mentioned, here is a list of some of the miscellaneous gear. It is offered here only as a check list:

Lip balm for windburned lips . . . beans, rice, canned corn, or other material for chumming a hole or brightening the bottom when spearing . . . ice cleats . . . a towel . . . handwarmers . . . extra gloves and socks . . . waterproof match holder . . . windproof cigarette lighter . . . lighter fluid . . . compass . . . transistor radio (to check on weather on big lakes) . . . binoculars . . . charcoal and burner . . . small heat stove . . . lantern . . . campstool or folding chair . . . tarp or heavy plastic for makeshift windbreaker . . . fifty feet of strong lightweight rope . . . sunglasses or tinted ski goggles . . . ice skates . . . small axe for cutting wood . . . knife . . . rods, tipups, and extra tackle . . . spud or auger . . . a file or stone for sharpening hooks . . . slush strainer or dipper . . . kerosene or other fuel for stove and lanterns . . . gaff hook . . . stringer or creel for carrying fish . . . barrel, box, or sled for gear . . . insulated

---

*During the 1975 Tip-Up-Town festival more than 25,000 people took part in the fishing fun.

jugs for hot soup, tea, or coffee . . . cooking and coffee-making utensils . . . whistle for signaling companions . . . litter bag . . . fish license and booklet of regulations . . . tool kit (if using a snowmobile) . . . spare spark plug, and drive belt for machines . . . lake bottom maps . . . insulated minnow bucket . . . small tin or discarded 35 mm. film can for carrying live, larvae baits . . . and CO_2 rescue packs (see the chapter "safety on the ice").

three

safety on the ice

The best ice fishing comes very early in the season, just after the lakes and rivers freeze over, and very late, about the time the ice becomes dangerous. We can still take advantage of these fish-biting times if we understand the ice and if certain precautions are followed.

As the temperature drops below 32 degrees Fahrenheit,

the surface water becomes "heavier" or more dense than the water deeper in the lake. It sinks, we might say. This pattern continues until the density is uniform, and then the top water begins to freeze into ice. This is one reason the very large, deep lakes are the last to freeze over.

Early bird ice fishermen get very nervous about this time, but caution is the word now. That first ice may look good, clear and solid, but, as a rule of thumb, it should be more than four inches thick before it will support you safely.

factors affecting ice strength

When the temperature continues to drop, after a lake is frozen over, the ice may boom or crack along the shoreline because of pressures. The shore ice is being pushed outward and upward and almost always is the most dangerous part of the total ice surface, unless the lake is very large and deep. In this case, the center is the last part to freeze solid enough to support you. Fluctuating water levels also cause the shore ice to be unsafe. The water may drop, leaving the ice high and dry with no liquid beneath to give it strength. Inlets and outlets around the shore are also dangerous spots which should be skirted by the ice angler en route to the fishing grounds. Stumps, docks and other obstructions around the shallows also weaken the sheet of ice while at the same time attracting fish for some mysterious reason. The shifting, living ice weakens itself around these things. Beware, especially early and late in the season.

Winds are another influence on the strength of the ice. Deep lakes may remain open in the middle throughout the winter, while the shore ice is risky, and the middle

Beware of ice next to pilings like these. It will be weak because the ice expands and contracts. Follow "ice paths" like these two fishermen. *(Courtesy Michigan Department of Conservation)*

zone between the shore and center of the lake is the safest of all for the fisherman. Remember the ice is lighter than the water. It floats. Water gives it support. Each winter it is common for some ice fishermen to become trapped on ice floes which break away from the shore and drift out into the big lakes.

In short, the fisherman on a medium to small inland lake, where most of our winter angling is done, will be safe if he uses his long-handled ice spud or chisel to check the ice ahead of him as he walks. He should rap it as he goes and occasionally cut a hole to examine the thickness. Of course, the follow-the-leader philosophy works best. If other anglers have been traveling a certain route from the landing or parking area out to the fishing grounds, they are doing it for a reason—that's the safe route.

A few yards from such an "ice road" there may be a strong current which has weakened the ice. From the surface, it may appear to be just like any other part, but natives will know it is there, and they will avoid such spots. Underwater springs, with flowing water, will also cause weak spots by keeping the water circulating. This will be a dangerous spot. Ironically it will also be a good fishing spot too. That moving water will contain a higher ratio of dissolved oxygen which will attract fish at this time of year. Moving water also acts as a smorgasbord of fish foods.

While the majority of ice fishermen will hit the lakes and ponds, there is considerable sport on streams and rivers. The rule is to avoid the swift water because the ice will be the thinnest here. Many fast streams will be open all winter long while ice forms quickly on sluggish rivers in the same area. Remember to check the ice each time out. Safe ice today may be a trap tomorrow because of temperature changes, chemicals in the water, snow cover, sunshine, shifting currents, ice fatigue, and other factors which all bear on the strength of ice.

Strong sunlight shining through the ice and reflecting back up off the sand or rock bottom will warm the ice from beneath and cause deterioration. This is difficult to detect, and your best defense is to keep a sharp eye out for discoloration in the ice. Heavy snow over the ice will insulate it against the cold and this may be another trouble spot. It may be clear, dry, and fluffy white on the top but it may be slushy and dangerous beneath.

Look out for man-made hazards. Thoughtless fishermen might drill a large hole and leave it as an unmarked trap. Though you may not go all the way in, you might break a leg. Unattended fishing holes should be marked with an evergreen limb, block of ice, or some other marker. In short, be suspicious of any change in the continuity of the ice or the color of it.

The U.S. Army Corps of Engineers, in an effort to learn more about ice, formed an organization called SIPRE, which stands for Snow, Ice, Permafrost Research Establishment. It was located at Wilmette, Illinois. SIPRE conducted much research and published some technical papers on these topics.

The strength or bearing capacity of ice is not based solely on the fact that ice is lighter than water, but on its resistance to bending under a load. That bearing capacity of ice is substantially higher than the load that produces the first cracking sounds. Regarding ice strength, which is of vital importance to ice fishermen, ice boaters, skaters, and others, SIPRE found that you can't always tell the strength of ice just by its looks or its thickness, or the daily temperature, or whether or not ice is covered with snow. The strength of the ice, therefore, depends on all these key factors, plus a number of others, including the depth of the water under the ice and local climatic factors that vary considerably from place to place.

Keep in mind that new ice is much stronger than old ice. Ice formed by direct freezing of lake or stream water will be stronger than ice formed from melting snow or than refrozen ice, or than ice made of water that bubbles up through cracks and then freezes on the surface. In other words, clear new ice is stronger than ice clouded with air bubbles. Four or five inches of this clear, new ice will be stronger than a foot of old or "rotten" ice.

driving and parking on ice

Most of us think of ice as brittle or like crystal. As indicated earlier, good ice is elastic. You may recall those days when you jumped up and down on a puddle of water with a very thin layer of ice over it. Remember how much jumping it took before you broke the ice? The same is true with good ice on a lake or river. It bends, gives, and bounces back, but it also fatigues if pressure, like that from a parked car, is on it for a long time. SIPRE found that vehicles should be moved around to alternate parking spots so that the ice can recover its earlier, normal shape and strength. The Army found a car parked on a foot of ice will depress that ice about one inch in a saucer-shaped area 200 feet in diameter. In other words, cars parked close together on such ice may increase the weight enough to pass the point where it will do any more bending.

SIPRE warned that cars may break through ice if the ice already has some scars or cracks in it. Drive across these refrozen cracks at right angles, and then be sure not to stop or park near such breaks.

Drivers should also be aware of resonance waves or ripples of vibration emanating from the automobile's motion over the ice. An exaggeration of these waves would be to liken them to the motion of a bull whip. The sheet of ice bends and waves up and down as the weight of the car moves across it. One certain speed is called the critical speed which is the danger point as we will explain.

The critical speed may crack this ice, but driving either slower or faster will substantially reduce the danger of cracking. Going faster than the critical speed risks losing control and running into a fishing hole, ice shanty, or another vehicle. Driving slower than the critical speed is recommended. Never drive close to another moving car because, according to SIPRE research, the resonance waves or ripples caused by the moving vehicles will clash and could cause a break in the ice. Here are the critical speeds for different depths: over 4 feet of water, travel at speeds slower than 9 mph; over 6 feet of water, 11 mph; 8 feet of water, 12 mph; 10 feet of water, 14 mph; 15 feet of water, 17 mph; 20 feet of water, 19 mph; and 30 feet of water, 22 mph. No critical speeds are available for snowmobiles, which weigh several hundred pounds, compared to several thousand pounds for a car, but the ice should be at least six inches thick and of good quality, before you venture out with a snowmobile onto a frozen lake or river.

Rule of thumb: drive around 5 mph until you know you are on solid ice over deep water.

This is an "ice buggy," an old car with chains and stripped of its cab to cut down weight. The unlucky fisherman hit a soft spot in the ice and broke through. (*Courtesy Michigan Department of Conservation*)

mud and snow tires

Conventional tire chains are fine for traction, but they are a bother to put on and they give a bumpy, noisy ride. Mud and snow tires, at present, are your best bet. They are fine for driving from home to the lake and adequate on the ice itself. Removing some of the air from each tire will give a little more traction even if they are shiny and bald. The softer tire will spread out more and grip the frozen surface. Remember to inflate the tires to the recommended pressure before hitting the open road after your fishing trip.

Driving on ice is always dangerous, no matter what the thickness of the ice or how many others are doing it. Most insurance companies have clauses which excuse them from liability if a car is lost in the water in this manner. Even if a car is only stuck nose down in the ice, most road service insurance will not cover such "off the highway driving." In some cases, ice fishermen use old junk cars for this very limited amount of winter travel on the ice, but even here there is the expense of removing the car from the lake. It can be costly even if the car cost practically nothing to begin with. Most states will not allow such littering of their lakes with old cars—even new cars.

escaping from submerging cars

If you must drive out on ice, then you must break one of the safety rules of the open highway—the rule of always wearing safety belts. *Don't wear them on the ice.* Be prepared to bail out—*pronto!*

Our studies on this subject and our experience have resulted in these suggestions: drive with all the windows rolled down and the doors ajar. Remember the resonance tables and drive slower than the critical speed. Keep a screwdriver or some other sharp object handy. If you start to break through, kick the transmission into neutral and bail out immediately.

Now, let's elaborate a little. Electric windows won't work in a car under water or even partially submerged. If your doors become stuck or jammed by the ice or water pressure, there may be no time to roll down a window to escape. Certainly some air will be trapped in if the windows are all up and the doors are closed, but your aim is to get out, not to keep the air in. The little air in the car will not mean much regarding flotation of a vehicle en route to the lake bottom. Another reason for the doors ajar: they may prevent a complete breakthrough by catching on the edge of the ice. Going in sideways is very infrequent. If a break should come at the side, the car will quickly right itself and not roll because there will always be some air around the inside of the roof. If you are driving a convertible, the best advice is to put the top down. The air trapped in your own clothes will more than bob you away from such a sinking automobile.

In examining state police records of cars going through the ice, we found most do not plunge like a rock. The ice usually gives under the front end where the vehicle is heaviest (except in rear engine sports cars). Troopers reported there was almost always a moment or two when alert ice fishermen could *dive* out across the ice, away from the break. Kicking the car into neutral prevents the rear wheels from driving the car all the way through a break.

Police reported that the fatalities usually come, not in

Partially submerged auto. Most cars sink nose first, like this one. *(Courtesy Michigan Department of Conservation)*

the initial sinking, but in the panic which follows. Fishermen get out but they don't know how to get back onto the ice. They should try standing on the top of their submerged vehicle, if it is in shallow water. They should also have some sharp instrument like a screwdriver, keys, or even a belt buckle to dig into the edge of the ice and hold on.

rescuing yourself and others

Nature tempts us early and late each ice fishing season by serving up some of the best fishing at these most dangerous times. During these periods of newly formed ice and very old, rotten ice, the risk of taking the dip fully bundled in heavy winter clothes is most critical.

And a dunking can come so quickly, you don't have time to bat an eye. I know. It happened to me once and I hope it never happens again. My unexpected swim came one February on a small trout fishing lake because I broke one of the most important rules—I failed to check the ice myself with a spud. There was rotten ice beneath a warm blanket of snow. One step from solid ice into the snow and—splash!

In struggling in the water I made another error. A fisherman will almost always bob to the surface, thanks to the air trapped inside his clothing. This happened to me, but in thrashing around trying to get out without help, this air had escaped and my clothing soon became water-soaked. It was like a suit of armor. I made still another mistake. I tried to keep my head, arms, and shouders high out of the water. This was foolish, because soaked clothes do not weigh anything as long as they are down in the water. It was only necessary to keep my face above water.

Should the bottom part beneath you, try to remember to remain calm—something very difficult to do, but easy to say. Concentrate your attention on holding to the edge of the solid ice. If it breaks away, make another grab in that same spot. Keep this up until you reach firm ice.

DUNKING TESTS. After that scary experience, we made some tests in a heated swimming pool by jumping and diving into the water with different types of ice fishing clothes on. It should be admitted that reactions are different in a heated pool. In the ice water, the shock of that water hitting your warm body really takes your breath away. Your hands seem to swell and fingers all become thumbs.

This is why we do not recommend trying to untie boot laces or buckles in the water. When walking to and from your fishing spot, boots should be loose so that if you should fall in, the boots can be kicked off underwater. Also, loose boots allow air to circulate around the feet so they do not perspire, only to quickly get cold when you stop walking.

In the heated pool we learned that a person entering the water feet first always will bob up quickly because of the air between his layers of clothing. As we said— but it is important to repeat—struggling causes this air to escape and hastens soaking. And wool sucks up water like a million soda straws.

In our tests we found that the best outfits to trap and hold air pockets are those with the hardest finish. Rubberized parkas are tops if they are zipped tight. The canvas windbreakers, though not as good as the rubber outfits, are much better than the one-piece coveralls with nylon finishes. Coverall suits, in turn, rank between the canvas windbreakers and the old-fashioned wool suits, which were the poorest floaters in our tests. Of course, some people swear by Army surplus flight suits and duck coats.

With all the different outfits, we were able to stay up longer and with very little effort provided: (1) the plunge was feet first, (2) we did not struggle or try to swim far, (3) we kept everything zipped or buttoned up tight, (4) arms were kept down in the water to prevent air loss, (5) we did not waste time and energy trying to get boots off, and (6) we did not try to ride high in the water.

A friend of mine once broke through and told me later the thing that bothered him the most was that he bumped his head on the bottom of the ice when he bobbed back up. Another ice fisherman told me his only problem, after getting dried out, was that his side hurt. In falling, he banged his side on the ice. All of us members of the "Polar Bear" club agreed that once the ice goes, a fisherman should just let himself go, relax, and try to go in feet first. But as we said, sometimes it breaks apart so fast he's in the drink before he realizes what's happening.

WHAT THE VICTIM SHOULD DO. Let's assume you have not knocked yourself out by bumping your head on the ice and are bobbing in open water, surrounded by rotten or cracked ice. What do you do? Besides praying, you should try to remain calm. Chances are someone nearby has heard the ice break or your cries for help. While waiting for assistance, hold onto the edge of the solid ice but do not attempt to pull yourself up if there is any chance of help getting to you soon. Your strength to keep your head above water is critical at a time like this. Don't waste it.

If you are wearing a CO_2 flotation device, this is time to trigger it. There are many CO_2 cartridge devices for sale, but none is approved by the U.S. Coast Guard, because the cartridges are not 100 per cent dependable.

Best CO_2 devices available are those used by serious scuba divers to bring them up from the depths. These have two cartridges fitted into the necks of a contraption resembling a football bladder and made of heavy-duty rubber. Lightweight plastic bladders with single CO_2 cartridges are the poorest made and least dependable. They only give the fisherman a false sense of security. Don't use them.

If you carried that rope over your shoulder, as was recommended in the chapter, "shelters, equipment, and accessories," this is the time to toss it to your would-be rescuer. Should a fisherman break through while alone on the ice, he can get out alone if he remains calm and doesn't struggle. His first problem is to get a grip on the edge of the ice. A tool, such as a belt buckle, car keys, knife, or some other sharp object, helps to dig into the ice.

If the luckless fisherman has obeyed earlier rules, he should have nothing tied on his back or roped to him. Remember, he should have been towing his tackle on a sled so this weight now cannot act as an anchor on him.

The accident victim should work on the thickest part up until he is far from the original break or he might fall up some momentum, he can roll up onto the ice and away from the break. Again, he should be careful not to stand up until he is far from the original break or he might fall through once more.

Never walk to a victim who has fallen through. Spread out and try to reach him with a board, branch, coat or some other handy item. (*Courtesy Michigan Department of Conservation*)

And since accidents always happen to "the other guy," here are some instructions which hold true, if you are the one making the rescue instead of the one being rescued.

WHAT THE RESCUER SHOULD DO. Keep back from the crack, or, in trying to give the dunked party a hand, you may be joining him in the drink. Use that rope. If you forgot the rope, use your coat or parka to reach the person in the water while lying spread eagle on the ice as the Red Cross safety instructors recommend.

Chances are you won't be able to get to a step ladder or a long board to use in the rescue, so remember the rope, coat, parka, belt, or even your fishing rod when trying to reach the unlucky fisherman.

The American Red Cross instructions on life saving and water safety cover many of the same points already mentioned, but let's run down the procedure once again:

1. To reach the victim, never walk to the break. Spread out flat on the ice.

2. Move slowly with a board, branch, ice sled, rope, or some other improvised device to reach the victim. If nothing can be found, several people can form a human chain with each person lying flat.

3. The victim should not try to shed his boots or coat, if it means releasing his grip on solid ice. There is a chance underwater currents may pull him under the solid ice and away from the break.

4. Once the victim is reached, he should help his rescuers by trying to float horizontally and use a flutter or frog kick to assist in pushing himself onto the ice.

5. The victim and his rescuer or rescuers should roll or crawl slowly back toward shore or safe ice many, many

yards before attempting to stand. Even then, they should not gang up and concentrate their combined weight in a small area.

6. Back on shore or at a fishing shelter, remove the wet clothing as soon as possible and briskly rub down the victim to speed up circulation. Of course, get him indoors or to a warm fire.

The Red Cross has a safety film on this subject, but it may not be available at all local chapters. It was made primarily for ice skaters, but most of the information applies to fishermen as well.

The very latest and best clothing for ice fishermen, as mentioned on page 24, are the flotation suits and jackets. They are available today in one-piece "snowmobile" suits or in two-piece pants and coats.

Although expensive, they are absolutely foolproof when it comes to floating all day in icy water. Some of the clothing is even U.S. Coast Guard-approved, in a class with life jackets. Some of the coats and suits we experimented with are bulky and expensive—usually over $100.00. The outfits were first manufactured for off-shore oil rig workmen, but were quickly adopted by the safety-minded ice fishermen.

four

All over North America, every ice fisherman has one thing in common—a hole in the ice, which makes him a still fisherman in the truest sense. He is confined to working out the area directly beneath him, and the smart angler realizes that fish are sluggish in the cold water and that where he places his hole is most important. He can drill more holes, and should, if action is slow, but this takes time and effort.

67

Assuming that he is dressed properly and knows more about ice safety, here are some preliminary steps an ice fisherman should take to shorten the time between catches.

getting started

In the beginning before he ever leaves home a winter fisherman should watch his local newspaper for reports that the ice is thick and the fish are biting. He should note which lakes are producing and keep a record. From year to year, this won't change much. If the newspaper is not one of the better ones with good outdoor news, then the angler has to do some checking on his own. State conservation departments have game wardens or fish wardens scattered around every state. These gents are very cooperative in passing out information when Cold-fanny Lake is producing. Information from such public officials is usually more reliable than data from a boat livery operator, bait dealer, or some local chamber of commerce. These types have a direct financial interest in getting ice fishermen to their lake or specific area around a lake. There are more than six million ice fishermen in North America who spend many, many millions of dollars every winter. Local businessmen want some of this business and have a tendency to color fishing reports.

So you pick an area with several lakes. Now, the best thing to do is drive by all the lakes and note where the most fishermen are set up for action. Chances are that's the hot spot for that particular time of year and time of day. Fishermen never are evenly spread over a lake, because the fish are never "all over." The fish caught in

Spread out to cover more territory. These anglers are using tipups and handlines to catch their trout. *(Courtesy Michigan Tourist Council)*

winter—primarily perch, bluegills, crappies, Northern pike, walleyes and the different trout—usually concentrate in areas of good food, cover, and oxygen. More about these later. Just remember the early fishermen are in an area because the fish are there, but this doesn't mean you should "horn in" and crowd someone who got there first.

finding your own spot

On a lake without other anglers, there are a few things you can do on your own to get started. Study a lake bottom map which will show the contour of the basin, its sand bars, weed beds, deep holes, dropoffs and, sometimes, underwater springs. These are usually available from the state conservation or fisheries department, local bait dealers, or chambers of commerce. Locally produced maps often will have areas marked where different fish normally hang out.

After examining the map, use your compass to strike out in the right direction until you feel you are at the dropoff, normally a good place to begin. Drill the first hole on the shore side of the dropoff. If there is no action, stretch out on the ice, place your face down next to the water, and cover your head with a coat. A bottomless bucket helps cut down the light so you can study the world under the ice. Look for those weeds and other obstructions mentioned above, because this is the best place to be. Small bait fish need this cover, and the game fish you're after will be nearby. And keep in mind winter fish are sluggish, since their cold-blooded functions are greatly reduced. You must be very close to them with the bait or lure most of the time. They need comparatively little food in winter, so meals served up on a hook must be expertly dished out.

winterkill

Certain shallow lakes which are dark under water because snow and ice cut off the sunlight have a winter die-off of fish called "winterkill." This occurs because aquatic plants cannot get the sunlight to produce oxygen, which is needed by the fish to keep healthy and active. In such a lake, holes in that ceiling of ice act as magnets to oxygen-hungry fish. Also vital in such a lake is the underground spring which injects fresh oxygen. Fish will congregate around these springs, a good place to catch them.

Winterkill might also occur in a bay which is part of a large lake. Although oxygen is one of the two elements of water (H_2O), gill-breathing animals are unable to use it in this form. It is the gaseous form of oxygen, dissolved in water, that they need. Usually lakes and streams contain an adequate though varying supply of the vital gas.

Other gases might contribute to winterkill. High concentrations of such gases as carbon dioxide and hydrogen sulfide are lethal to fish, and a considerable buildup of these often accompanies water stagnation in the winter.

Winterkills occur mostly in lakes less than fifteen feet deep, although those shallow bays just mentioned may also suffer. Fish in lakes with too much vegetation and mucky bottoms are more apt to suffer than those in lakes with only moderate amounts of rooted vegetation. The bottom soils of the latter are largely inorganics such as marl, sand, gravel, or rock.

Some fish require more oxygen than others. Northern pike, perch, pumpkinseed, sunfish, and bullheads can exist on less oxygen than bass and bluegills, which are called bream or brean in some regions of the country. When oxygen depletion reaches the critical point, many bass and bluegills die, while these other fish pull through. Lakes with annual winterkill problems are often opened by state officials to "no limit" fishing. Watch for announcements in your local paper.

looking into holes

Usually a five- or six-inch hole in the ice is adequate. A four-incher is probably enough for all panfishing. If you find a lake where panfish won't fit, nose up, through a four-inch hole, drop me a line, and we'll fish it together.

If snow and slush are piled around a hole, it helps block out the light. Such a hole looks like a miniature volcano. There are several gimmicks in sports shops, which resemble a canvas cylinder, designed to rest over the hole and keep ice from forming. This crust of new ice will freeze your bobber and cause you to miss bites. Another gadget is a small metal cup which fits in the hole at the water line and clamps to the ice. In the cup, two or three small charcoal lumps burn and keep the water warm.

Graphite and a number of chemicals like alcohol, antifreeze and glycerine compounds are often used to retard freezing in the hole, but such de-icers taint the water, and the experienced ice fishermen don't bother with them, because they keep fish away. Of course, the very best way to keep ice from forming is to keep the traffic moving through the hole—keep the fish coming up.

hole primers

After fifteen minutes of no action, moving to another spot is the smartest thing to do, but before moving, there are a few things worth trying to speed the action. This is called priming a hole. Crushed eggshells are popular. If there are a few hard-boiled eggs in your lunch, use the shells after crushing them between your hands to sparkle up a dull hole. The pieces twist and flash in the light as they flutter down, occasionally attracting fish immediately. If they don't come in at the moment, don't despair. Fish may become curious with all that material on the bottom and move in to investigate. Usually the shell chips attract minnows, and the larger fish come after the minnows.

If you don't care to eat eggs just to get the shells, try oatmeal, which has been known to attract bait fish, as well as the larger pickerel and perch. Other chumming material includes canned corn, split peas, white baking beans, cornmeal, cracker crumbs, rice, and some of the leafy breakfast foods. Farina is another good chum material, but it becomes mushy on the bottom in a short time. A couple more: ground clamshell or confetti.

Another trick is to take the first fish caught—or borrow one from a neighboring angler—and scale it over the open hole which, by the way, should have been cut so the bottom is larger than the top, like an inverted funnel. After scaling a fish, gut it out and drop the innards down the hole. The fluids will excite larger predatory fish like walleyes, pike, and muskellunge. The eyeball of a perch makes a terrific natural lure for panfish, but more on that later in the chapter, "baits for fish, large and small."

A tip to speed up the action: lower a larger minnow on one line and then work a panfish lure, wiggler, or corn borer on another line. The large minnow, rigged with a tiny wire just under the top or dorsal fin, works like a decoy to attract panfish you're trying to catch.

Don't overlook holes abandoned by earlier anglers. Remember fish move about. A dead well today might be a gusher tomorrow. In digging your own holes, pick your spot carefully, keep it clean of ice and slush, and always make sure the edges are smooth, so the line will not become frayed on the sharp edges.

Keep in mind a little flash, a little chum, and a little thinking can go a long way toward enticing reluctant fish. If they weren't a little reluctant, what fun would there be in outsmarting them?

five

Ice fishing success is determined, more than any other single factor, by the item on or around the hook which is supposed to make the fish bite. These enticers fall into two major categories, the live or natural baits and the artificials, lures and flies. This chapter deals with the live baits, or baits which were once alive, and natural food. It also deals with some foods not commonly eaten by fish, like cheese and marshmallows. We use the word "bait" to mean something the fish will or can eat and not simply mouth and then spit out.

If an angler were to be restricted to one type of bait for all his fishing. the smart fisherman would take the live minnow. "Minnow" has come to mean any small fish, but actually there is a minnow family of fishes, just as there are sunfish, salmon, pike, and other families of fishes. There are around 2,000 different species of minnows (*Cyprinidae*), and just about all of them never get more than a few inches long. Most notorious exception to this is the carp (*Cyprinus carpio*), the demon of the mud flats and warm shallow waters, who often grows to tremendous size. A carp weighing 86 pounds was caught in the Minnesota River by an angler identified as C. A. Cameron of Shakopee, Minnesota, in 1906.

The carp, an import from Asia and Europe, has terrible eating habits which destroy habitat for game fish and is considered an undesirable character by serious fishermen. This is why practically all the states and Canadian provinces specifically prohibit the use of carp minnows and goldfish as bait fish. If there were no such restrictions, anglers might allow live carp minnows to escape in other "clean" lakes and rivers, and in a few short seasons the carp would virtually take over the water. Bait dealers should recognize carp minnows and not sell them to any fishermen.

The same goes for goldfish. It is tempting to use goldfish for bait, because they are so colorful and long-lived on a hook. Better than use such a critter and risk the long-term destruction of fishing for years to come, stick with the harmless minnows such as the golden shiner, dace, and similar species. Smelt, with a schizophrenic reputation, is also illegal as a bait in some areas. Bowfins and suckers fall into this same group of shady characters and should be avoided, unless they are sliced into small strips, and some states even prohibit this.

The rule of thumb is to use a minnow which occurs naturally in the water you are fishing. And the bigger the minnow, the bigger the catch—most of the time.

chubs and shiners

Large shiners of five or six inches are good for Northern pike, walleyes, lake trout, whitefish, and muskies. Shiners in the one- to three-inch size serve well as crappie bait,

Small shiner hooked behind dorsal fin

and those around an inch or less do Spartan service on perch. They are raised commercially by minnow dealers or trapped under permit and are probably found over more of the North American ice fishing range than any other live minnow bait.

The creek chub rarely grows as large as the largest golden shiner, but he is a good bait fish, because he seems to be tougher on the hook and in the minnow pail. He is known by many different names, which include horned dace, common chub, and Northern creek chub. He usually can be purchased from bait dealers where you plan to fish.

Ice skimmer and bait pail *(Courtesy New York Department of Conservation)*

In the summer, the heat kills minnows. In the winter, the cold is the minnow's enemy and yours. There are some things that can be done about this. Keep them warm by placing the minnow bucket next to the lantern or heater in your ice sled. Or the minnow bucket can be put inside the car, if you drive on the ice. On the ice, pack snow around the bucket to insulate it. It is not uncommon to see a minnow bucket, with a lid on top, lowered into a large hole in the ice and held up by a rope or a stick through the handle.

Old-fashioned metal buckets are the most rugged on the market, but the modern sponge plastic or sponge rubber bucket is made of material that not only "breathes" but is better insulation against the cold. These newer minnow buckets are also excellent in the summer. If you already have a metal minnow bucket, paint it black or some other dark color, so that it will absorb the sun's rays and retain some of the heat. One source suggested a shot of de-icing whiskey in the bucket will not only keep the minnows alive, but very happy. This is hearsay and has not been tested.

Because live minnows are the most valuable, they should be the last item obtained when preparing for an ice fishing outing. Gather all other gear and make all preparations before purchasing your live bait. If there is a long drive involved between the fishing grounds and the bait dealer, there is danger to the minnows in the car. To aerate the minnow bucket, put a small rubber hose in the bottom of the bucket and the other end up to the car window. Wind up the window enough to hold the hose in place. As the car moves forward, a stream of fresh air will be sent down through the hose to keep the water in the minnow bucket moving. Minnows can be kept alive indefinitely this way.

Fishermen kill more minnows than they help by changing water too often. Fresh water, full of dissolved oxygen, is fine if the temperature is very close to the water the fish are used to. The shock of going from warm water into cold water knocks the life out of the friskiest minnow.

hooking a minnow

But it is possible to keep minnows alive on the hook by inserting the point properly. Assume we have our minnows alive and frisky out on the ice. To get one without wetting fingers or gloves, use a small strainer swiped from the kitchen. If this handy item is left inside the minnow bucket, it won't freeze or get lost easily in the snow or on the ice. And it beats getting your hands wet every time you need a fresh minnow. A wiggly minnow between cold fingers is a difficult thing to hold without squeezing the minnow too hard while trying to get the hook in.

Use those cheap cloth work gloves you should have packed. The cloth, coarse as it is, makes it possible to hold the minnow without crushing him. Once baited up, drop these gloves into your ice sled, where they will stay warm and dry near the lantern or portable heater, and slip into your warmer, better quality, wool gloves and big mittens.

The best way to hook a live minnow, and for good reason, is just under and slightly behind the fin on the back. The hook should not be at right angles to the minnow. Angle it back so that the shank and point of the hook are aimed toward the tail. This hooking method allows a Northern pike to swallow the bait head first with the hook, before he realizes there is a string attached to this offering. Some claim it doesn't make a real hoot of a difference because, they say, the pike comes in and chomps down on the minnow from the side. He's going to get hooked either way—we hope.

Hook a dead minnow through both eyes or lips. A third hookup method is through the tail. A tail hookup,

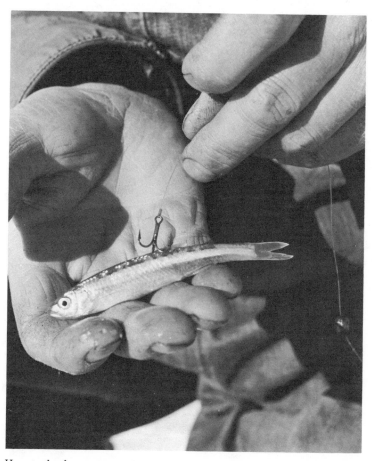

How to hook a minnow *(Courtesy Michigan Department of Conservation)*

with the sinker, line, etc., trailing behind, inhibits the bait's movement. He tires quickly and becomes unattractive to a passing fish. On the other hand, a tail-hooked bait certainly does have the "injured minnow" look which works well in the summer. But we lean toward the active look a good, healthy, wiggling minnow gives.

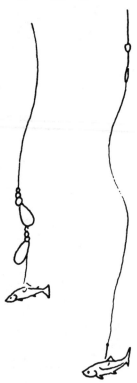

Live bait rigs *(Courtesy New York Department of Conservation)*

One way to give a dead bait "life" is jigging him up and down. Give him the "twitch," a quick jerk up by flipping the rod tip, etc. Now, raise the line above your head rapidly and let it slowly back down. As it returns, keep the line fairly taut. Note the feel of the natural flutter of the dead bait as it sinks like a leaf swinging down from a tree in autumn. You will get many strikes on the down-flutter. This is the reason for the line without too much slack. Be ready for a strike. Dead minnows can also be made to flutter by stuffing a small split shot weight in their mouths and then hooking them through the lips. Now raising and lowering the rod causes the head to come up and then dive, and the rest of the minnow's natural anatomy goes to work for you. When there is a choice, however, always use the live bait, saving the dead ones for when the action picks up. The school psychology takes over down under the ice, and anything that looks good gets snapped up by one fish greedy enough to bite just so his pal won't get the minnow. Fish are just like people in some ways. The chapter, "ice fishing flies and lures" deals with using live or natural baits in combination with the hardware lures.

worms

While minnows and lively smelt may be tops for the big ones like the trout, walleye, pike, muskie, and whitefish, small wormy, creepy, crawly creatures are the T-bone steaks of the bluegill and other panfish set. Such baits are the same kinds of things that would make a woman scream if she saw one on her lapel or a man step on if he were not an ice fisherman. They are the corn borers, insect larvae, grubs, maggots, meal worms and wigglers, just to name the more popular items.

What about plain old worms? Fine, if you can find them when it is zero outside. Actually, worms are not the top bait with winter fishermen, because they don't

Manure worm

rate very high with fish in the winter. Worms are not abundant under the ice. In fact, they are just not there, and fish know that. Certainly, they will take fish, if

Nightcrawler

small segments are used on the tip of a tiny hook. If one insists on using worms through the ice, he should stick with the small angleworms or small segments of night crawlers. Those who plan ahead cache quantities of worms in the fall by keeping them in a wooden bucket or earthenware crock filled to within a few inches of the top with a rich loam. This is excellent conditioner for worms.

Because of the trouble of getting, keeping, and feeding worms before they can be used, insect baits are far more popular with ice fishermen. Just in the past few years, ice fishing has become so popular, there has sprung up a vast winter bait industry which in some spots is more valuable to resort community economy than the summer bait business. Bait dealers don't make a nickel from water skiers, motor boat hot rodders, swimmers, and waders, but the person who walks into his place after there is ice on the lake or river is a cash customer who needs bait.

insect baits

Knowing what fish naturally feed on under the ice is the real key to successful fishing here. This knowledge makes the difference when the action is slow, while on the other hand, practically anything will bring them to hook when "the bite" is on. One way to find out what fish are eating is to open the stomach of the first one caught and examine the contents. However, this is not as easy as it sounds for a fisherman, untrained in biology, out there in the cold. Even for a trained eye, it is not easy to identify the different larval forms.

DRAGONFLIES. In an article in the *Wisconsin Conservation Bulletin*, Roland B. Stewart, forest entomologist, and Leonard J. Druschba, district fish manager, give a good rundown on the real McCoys and the very good substitutes. First of the "McCoys" are the dragonflies *(Odonata)*, best known of the insects because of their size and rapid darting flight. They are harmless to man, in spite of antiquated beliefs to the contrary. In fact, their mosquito-eating habit makes them very beneficial. These broad and flat nymphs are best caught by a seine or dip net. They are cannibalistic.

MAYFLIES. Mayflies *(Emphemeridae)* are delicate net-winged insects with two or three hairlike tails. The nymph stage is an excellent fish food. When ice fishermen talk about wigglers, they usually mean mayfly nymphs. Because these are so important to fish, it may be illegal in

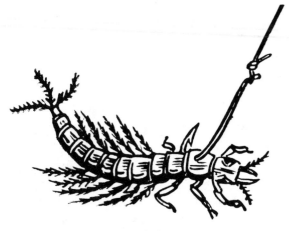

Mayfly larva

your area to dig mayflies. Mayflies live in all fresh, unpolluted water and adapt to a great diversity of habitat. The short-lived adults are commonly called "drakes" and "fishflies," and there are over 500 different species in the United States and Canada. The important nymphs as baits are usually 1½ to 2½ inches long. They burrow into the mud.

To spot a mayfly nymph, look for its long, feathery gills, which are arranged in pairs along the back and sides of the abdomen. The body terminates in three long tails. Each of its jaws is developed into a long, pointed tusk which aids the insect in burrowing. To capture the nymphs, use a fine screen to sift bottom material and be careful in handling them. They are delicate. After collecting, they should be put in a tank or aquarium with a layer of dead leaves and leaf mold on the bottom. Usually, lower water temperature will help them keep longer, especially if they are not crowded. Mayfly wigglers are excellent for bluegills, crappie, sunfish, and perch.

Caddis fly larva with sand casing

CADDIS FLIES. The caddis fly (*Trichoptera*) is mothlike and also common around water. The wings and body are usually hair-covered. Fish eat caddis flies as they crawl on the bottom, on rocks, or on vegetation. Excellent for bluegills, crappie, sunfish, and perch.

STONEFLIES. Stoneflies *(Plecoptera)* are also good winter baits, but difficult to keep on a hook because they are rather fragile. This species hides under leaves or rocks along streams and some rocky lake shores. Good for most panfish.

HELLGRAMMITES. The hellgrammite is the larval form of a large winged insect called the dobsonfly *(Corydalus cornutus)*, which often reaches three to four inches in length. The fly has large, lacy wings and hornlike jaws an inch long in the males and half as long in females. The

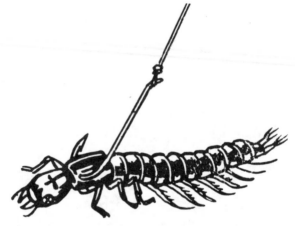

Hellgrammite

larva is found under rocks in great numbers in warm-water streams. They are aquatic carnivores, feeding on mayflies, stoneflies, and smaller insects. You can feed them hamburger in captivity. Hellgrammites can be identified easily by slender, fleshy appendages along their abdomens. They are tougher and more tenacious of life than may-flies and caddis flies. Some fishermen think hellgrammites are rather large for panfish but they are excellent for bass and other fish in this size group.

With snow and ice over everything when we want to go fishing, collecting natural baits like those just described is not easy. It can be done, but it is less trouble to find substitutes like the corn and wood borers, maggots, mousies, mealworms, leather jackets, and goldenrod gall worms. Good bait dealers will usually have all or most of these baits.

WOOD BORERS. Wood borers are small, white, round, segmented grubs—immature forms of beetles. The beetles lay eggs in the bark of dead or dying trees late in the spring and early in the summer. The young larvae bore in and feed just under the bark. In the fall you can find them deep in their wood galleries. Fire-killed pines are excellent places to find these grubs for ice fishermen interested in gathering their own borers. In September and October, the grubs can be easily found by peeling off loose bark. Later the trees must be split open to get them out. Actually, fishermen are doing foresters and lumbermen a service by taking these pests. They can also be found by splitting posts, railroad ties, mine props, and rotten logs. Sometimes they can be kept in sawdust until needed for panfishing.

GOLDENROD GALL. Another good substitute food is the larva from the round goldenrod gall. This is a small white maggot, the immature form of a pretty brownish fly with banded wings *(Eurosta solidaginis)*. These flies, in May and June, lay their eggs on the stems of the goldenrod. As the larvae develop, the plant tissue forms a gall. It is one of nature's mysteries how the insect controls this abnormal growth of the plant tissue so that the galls are always the same shape for this species. The maggot hibernates in the gall during the winter. This is where the ice fisherman finds his waiting bait. The round gall is the one with the bait inside. The oblong gall, formed by another insect, is empty. That insect has already matured and left. When you collect the galls, break or cut them off and leave them in one piece for storage in a cold place until needed. Since these larvae are small, several on a hook are often used at one time.

MIGHTY MOUSIES. Mousies are so named because of their mouselike bodies and tails. They are the immature form of the syrphus fly *(Syrphidae)*, a yellowish, banded bee-like fly which is often seen hovering around flowers in

Mousie *(Courtesy Michigan Department of Conservation)*

warm weather. The larvae feed on decaying vegetable matter, and are often found in rotten wood, mud, water, or decomposing material. The tail is actually a breathing tube and is telescopic. Mousies are tough. A good one might last an ice fisherman all day.

MEALWORMS AND CORN BORERS. Mealworms are also rather hard. They are waxy, yellow, round worms which may reach an inch in length. They are immature black beetles which feed on grain, flour, and meal—common pests around feed mills and granaries. It is easy to rear them and they make a handy source of panfish bait.

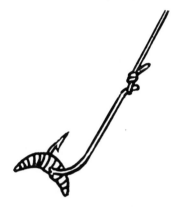

Mealworm

The corn borer is still another larva, which can be found by splitting open standing corn stalks in winter. Take your pick.

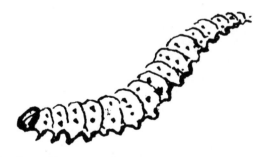

Corn borer (*Courtesy Michigan Department of Conservation*)

Most of these crawly things just described are tiny insect bombs which need only heat to trigger them into their larger stage of life. It is important that they be kept cold.

Small tin cans which once held 35 mm. film or 16 mm. movie film make handy containers for insect baits. Flip-top cigarette boxes also come in handy for this. The flat movie film cans are a favorite of many, because they can be slipped into an inside coat or shirt pocket, where body heat will keep the baits reasonably soft and flexible.

other natural baits

This section, because of their fish-catching qualities, includes some other natural food baits, such as salmon eggs, cheese, peas, canned corn kernels, marshmallows, and cut

Red and white salmon eggs

baits. Cut baits can be strips sliced from suckers, large chubs, or other fish, and then jigged on a handline to give them some movement and action. Anything a fish eats, might eat, or gets mad enough to bite on will fit in here.

One could ask how canned corn fits into this category. Corn certainly isn't a natural food, but it does resemble fish eggs—or a cluster of them, and it is therefore a "natural" imitation. In Alaska, canned small shrimp and salmon eggs are listed as the two most important ice fishing baits used. In British Columbia, where rainbow and Eastern brook trout, kokanee salmon, and char are the most important winter fish caught, most popular baits are worms, spinners, shrimp, kernels of corn, and bits of meat. If you can get a neighbor to let you catch roaches in his house, they make a good natural bait. So do crickets.

No matter what you have for bait, there are different techniques of manipulating the terminal tackle which will add to your success. The same goes for the other things mentioned earlier, like where to fish, how deep, when, etc. Keep all these things in mind, check with natives who know which baits or techniques are working at the time, and follow their suggestions. The angler ready to experiment and ask questions will get the jump on his stand-pat competitors.

Anyone using almost anything for bait can catch fish sometimes. But when the sun throws that last stream of light and then hides its face behind the horizon, and small fires and lanterns glow in flickering spots on the ice, the fellow who understands both his fish and his bait is the "lucky" one who takes home a good stringer of sweet panfish.

six

ice flies and lures

Modern ice fishermen who don't want to bother seeking live or natural bait for each trip are swinging over to the many artificial lures and flies. These include all the "phonies"—the imitations of natural fish food which are made out of wood, steel, chrome, nickel, feathers, rubber, plastics, and even glass. These, when designed and used properly, fool the fish into biting. Practically all these lures must be attended to, because the fish will reject them immediately. In other words, when fishing artificials, always keep the line or rod in hand to set that hook fast, or you'll lose your fish.

Jigging lure

Basically, the difference between artificial lures used in the winter and those used in the summer or in open water is that ice lures are designed to attract fish while being worked up and down. Warm weather lures are made to twist, flash, and wiggle deceitfully while being pulled horizontally through the water.

Russian hooks (*Courtesy Michigan Department of Conservation*)

Some lures may be used both through the ice and in open water in other seasons, and they have numerous trade names. Their general design is simple—they have a spoon shape with a hook fastened to the narrow end. These are called Russian hooks or jig spoons. At times, these will take perch, pike, walleyes, trout, muskies,

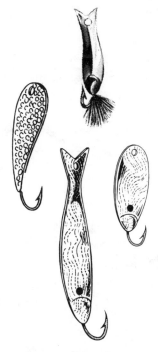

Detailed drawings of Russian hooks *(Courtesy Art Best, Sebewaing, Michigan)*

bass, and black and white crappies without any additional baits on the hook. Many use these spoons or Russian hooks with a dead minnow impaled crosswise on the hook or with a wiggler or other larvae. For every angler who endorses live and artificial combinations, there is one who will advise they should not be integrated.

secrets of an expert

There does seem to be general agreement that on the panfishes, combinations of natural bait with tiny teardrop hooks are best. One of the very best ice fishermen I knew fished with combination lures and baits so well he could catch perch and bluegills in a jigger of gin with his teardrop baited with white fly larvae. If he had any secrets worth disclosing they were these:

Teardrop hook (*Courtesy Michigan Department of Conservation*)

He fished the same two or three lakes all year, every year. He knew the bottoms. He knew where to go on different types of days and at different times during the season. (Usually shallow early, deep water midseason, and shallow again just before the spring breakup.) He varied the depth and always advised, "The proper depth is where the fish are." One thing, however, was consistent with this particular panfish expert: he always used the tiny teardrop hook with a mousey or white fly larvae. He said the color of a lure is just as controversial in the winter as in summer and that there is no "best" color for all ice fishing. Based on his personal records, the best indicator of success, the fluorescent or "fire" colors are

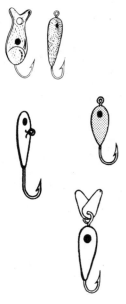

Ice fishing hooks *(Courtesy Art Best, Sebewaing, Michigan)*

most popular, because they catch the most fish. He favored yellow early in the season, shifting to green a little later for perch.

color, flash, and movement

A very popular small lure is pearl with red dot. Crappie fishermen prefer orange lures with small minnows. While color does seem to be very important, action is even more vital to success.

"Fire" colors are far from resembling the natural color of bait. They do bring the fish in by getting their attention, and, once in close, the fish usually take the hook because of the live bait on the point. Gaudy colors fail in milky water which is riled by winds or tides; when this happens, brass and copper lures are used. For reasons known only to the fish, they can see these lures better under adverse conditions. Brass and copper were the materials for the original "Russian hooks" mentioned earlier in this chapter.

Flasher *(Courtesy Michigan Department of Conservation)*

Flashing spoons are also used to attract fish to the vicinity of the hole. Some anglers use large, flashy spoons to lure fish and then do the actual catching on a smaller handline rig with live bait on a small hook. Today's well-made jigging spoon is weighted, usually by the solder which fastens the hook to the blade. The line is tied at the broad end so that the gadget hangs with the neck and hook at the bottom. A sharp twitch with your rod or wrist will shoot the spoon up, and then it will flutter and flash as it settles back down. It is a good practice at first to check out different lures in a bucket of water in order to develop the correct amount of snap and twitch to give them the ultimate action. Remember in all artificial lure and fly fishing in the winter, it is the action down below that counts.

Adding flash to the business end of the line is easy. Scrape the lead sinker with a pocket knife to get to the shiny part of that necessary item. Better yet, instead of a hunk of lead, use a highly polished stainless steel or silver-coated spoon with the hooks removed as a weight.

If you have a live minnow or golden shiner at the very end of the line, add flash by tying beads about two feet above the bait. Above the beads, attach a free-spinning flasher blade from an old fishing lure. This will flutter and spin as the bait is raised and lowered, giving more light-reflecting flash to the rig.

An on-the-ice trick: remove the silver paper from a cigarette pack or the foil from a chewing gum wrapper. Wrap this around the line about two feet from the hook and pinch it tight with your teeth to keep it from sliding down the line.

fly fishing in winter?

There was a time when only a few well-stocked sports and bait stores even bothered with wintertime lures and ice flies, but today with more than six million ice fishermen frolicking around all winter, practically every bait shop, department store, and sports counter is stocked with these important items.

Usually when a couple of anglers mention "fly fishing," it conjures up pictures of a lazy summer evening on a glassy-smooth bass and bluegill lake, where a fisherman with a nine-foot fly rod flicks and twitches his feathered deceit out on a hair-fine leader, barely making a ripple on the water. Or fly fishing means wading a giggling trout stream back in some green forest. Not so now. Ice fishermen have been using flies for about twenty years to take panfish. Proper flies in the hands of an experienced fisherman from late November until early April are just as effective as the most wiggling wigglers. In fact, the first ice fly patterns were tied to duplicate the action of wigglers. In those lazy summer months when there is no room for a fisherman on a motor boat-scuba diver-water skier-filled lake, he can retire to his air-conditioned den and tie flies for the winter fishing.

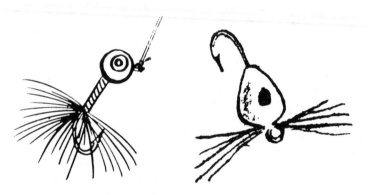

Ice flies (*Courtesy Michigan Department of Conservation*)

Take a No. 10 to 14 hook with a medium to long handle and squeeze on a tiny split shot on the hook's curve. Then build up the body with silk floss and make the wings out of soft hackle. Much easier, buy flies in different patterns until you find one which works for you and then tie your own duplicate.

Using a fly is also an art. In the chapter "baits for fish,

large and small," we recommended jigging and twitching the rod or line and then raising it an arm's length to get the right action. With flies, this operation is far more delicate. It is so gentle that in most cases the natural shiver of an angler's arm does the trick. The idea is to make those little wigglerlike flutters that say to the panfish, "Come and get it!" Panfish, while the ones which most likely will take a fly, are not alone. They may be accompanied to the fly gourmet table by larger fish like walleyes, Northern pike and even black bass.

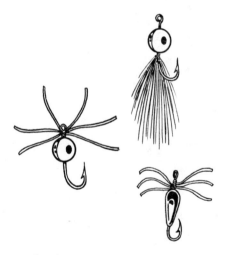

More ice flies *(Courtesy Art Best, Sebewaing, Michigan)*

There is no sharp distinction between a lure, a teardrop, and a fly in ice fishing, since some lures come with flashing blades, feathers, and other accessories like chrome and fox tails on automobiles. More and more of the small weighted and colored hooks are showing up on the counters with rubber "spider legs" and/or feathers and hackle. Somewhere in the artificial fraternity is the lead-headed jig—neither lure nor fly, but a year round fish-

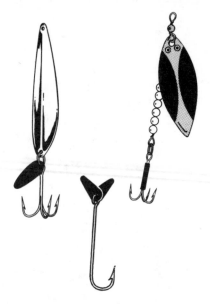

Ice jigs *(Courtesy Art Best, Sebewaing, Michigan)*

catcher. A jig is simply a weighted hook, brightly colored with some feather or hair for added flash and motion as it is raised and lowered sharply in the water.

plastic lures

In the early 1960's, fishermen started using, with some success, new plastic molded lures which looked like minnows, mousies, grubs, corn borers, and worms. One company even brought out a "raspberry ball," which does catch fish through the ice, although no fish normally eats raspberries. These so-called soft, flex, or "cream lures" of plastic and rubber work, but they need man-provided action to make them attractive. Some even have a delicious licorice scent which, in a weak, hungry moment out on the ice, may tempt you to take a bite yourself. The plastic salamanders, pollywogs, and tadpoles have the hooks right in them and some have weighted heads. Best feature of the large variety of "instant baits" is that there is never any danger of their freezing. In some of the homemade jigging rods, the handles are drilled out, so that many of these small plastics and other min-lures can be carried in the rod handles. Again it must be emphasized that such artificials are practically useless on a tipup or at the bottom of a line fastened to a bobber, unless they move.

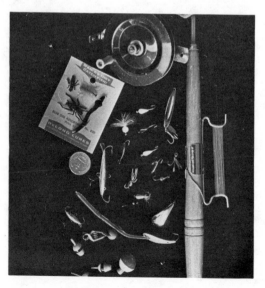

seven

how to catch panfish

Argue all you want, there are only two kinds of fish—big ones and little ones. In the very earliest days, big ones were taken through the ice, because they were larger targets for the trappers, Eskimos, Indians, and earliest New World settlers with their spears. Big fish, all kinds, were important in the winter, since they offered the most meat for the effort.

Smaller fish, the perch, smelt, bluegills, crappies, and the like, are really modern game for the winter fish hunter, since catching them means shifting the emphasis to sport. Those who seek pan-size critters are out for fun and sport first, and something for the table second. Most ice fishing in North America today, then, is for these panfish, which are found everywhere from the Atlantic across the northern half of the United States and all of Canada up to and including Alaska. They are the backbone of ice fishing.

the sunfish family

Judging from our survey of over thirty states and all Canadian provinces, members of the sunfish family are most often taken through the ice. There are thirty species in the sunfish clan, led by such scrappy smallfries as the common bluegill, rock bass, crappies, warmouth, and pumpkinseed. These are the more common names. Local names of some of these fish include just plain sunfish, Sacramento perch, goggle-eye, redeye, stumpknocker, mud bass, brim, bream or brean, copperhead, sun perch, green sunfish, longear sunfish, etc. Despite this confusion, they are all similar fish with a lot of aliases. The big boys of the sunfish family are the largemouth and smallmouth basses. Unfortunately, from the ice angler's viewpoint, they are relatively unimportant in the winter, because they are very inactive.

Largemouth bass, alias slough bass, Oswego bass, or green trout, is a creature of shallow, fertile, sluggish waters. Those small farm ponds, often overlooked by fishermen, will produce some big catches after the first ice forms in the late fall and early winter. He can be taken on ice flies, pieces of worm, larval and other insect lures in the winter.

The largemouth *(Micropterus salmoides)* will occasionally be caught on a pike fisherman's trap or tipup. His range is practically all of the ice fishing states and many parts of southern Canada, along the U.S. border. In our list of winter fish, as much as we love him in the summer on a quiet pond, he must get a low priority rating.

His cousin, the smallmouth *(Micropterus dolomieu),* likes cold, deeper water and can be taken through the ice on a variety of flies, hardware lures, and natural baits —and a lot of luck. Scientists don't know a powerful lot about the smallmouth in the winter, except that his activity is slowed down, and he retreats to the deepest holes in lakes and rapid rivers.

Now, let's meet the runts who make up an important part of the ice fisherman's catch. These are in the sunfish family. All of these fishes are shallow-water dwellers who do some moving to deeper holes, ten to thirty feet, but are most often found and caught in water less than ten feet deep. They are all schooling fish. Where there is one, there is usually a large congregation.

For an opener, start with a small hole about four inches across. Drill or chisel it along the edge of a weed bed where these fish will be hiding and feeding, or near some stump, dropoff or other "cover" where the fish live and feed. Keep the hole shaded with a box or small mound of snow to protect it from the wind and excess light. Rig a very light monofilament line, about two-pound test, or a light tippet from an old fly fishing leader with the most delicate balance between hook, sinker, and bobber, if a bobber is to be used at all.

There has been a trend to do away with sinkers and

use weighted hooks. These are "teardrops" of metal around the shanks of the hooks, which range from No. 4 up through No. 10 and 12 for panfish. The weighted portion is brightly colored and attractive enough in itself to catch fish without any bait. Some anglers stick a fish eye on the hook point and find this very deadly. The fish eye is impaled on the hook not through the dead center of the eye, but through and around the pupil to keep the fluids from escaping and to give the item more flash and flutter as it is sharply raised and lowered.

Without these rigs, a two-pound test transparent mono-filament line on a medium stiff rod about two and a half feet long does just as well. Anything longer forces you to stand that much farther away from the hole, and this is unnecessary. Using the line hand over hand is equally good for panfishing. Take this light line and tie a small hook, because panfish all have small mouths, to the very end. About a foot up the line, pinch on a small split shot. Simplicity is the key here.

The ice seals off the lake surface, where in the spring, summer, and fall panfish take food from the top. This ice, therefore, makes them primarily bottom feeders. This is where to go first with your presentation. Most of the action is from six inches to a foot and a half off the bottom. When fishing is slow, try other zones from the bottom up to the zone just beneath the ice itself. Panfish are dainty bait takers at this time. An inexperienced ice fisherman will not detect a bite, unless he knows how to spot the smallest movement of his bobber, which should be in eyelash balance with his sinker, hook, and bait. When this bobber does move, often sideways and not with that "plunk" downward as in the other seasons, the fisherman must be hair-trigger quick to set the hook sharply but without great force.

PUTTING THE BAIT TO WORK. The baits are basically small, wiggly things like maggots, white fly larvae, corn borers, mousies, wax worms, and mayfly wigglers, which are called Molly grubs in Canada. Wigglers should be hooked through the third segment from the end of the tail and in such a way that the stomach will be toward the bottom. Hooked this way, wigglers will live longer. One hooked through the front of the body or the head will fan itself to death. With mousies, which are popular because they are tough and long-lived, put two on the hook. Then squeeze the top one so that its body oils and juices will cover the lower mousey. The odor of these juices and oils will spread through the water and attract fish to the remaining one.

Jigging the bait up and down may turn the trick when action is slow. There are extremes in this which are just as bad as no bait movement at all. Always remember most fish are sluggish in winter. Panfishing jigging, therefore, is a short, snappy rod twitch and not the dramatic raising and lowering of the rod as is done for bigger species. Try to visualize the lure and/or bait combination as it appears to the reluctant panfish. One should even try this in a pitcher of water at home, so the action of any particular combination can be seen and understood. Here's how to go about the typical panfish jig: check the depth with a dropline and a weight to be sure you are beginning in that critical zone six to eighteen inches off the bottom. Next, let out enough fishing line after you are rigged up, so that when your rod is held horizontal, the business portion is in that fish-catching zone. Now, sharply raise, with a flick of the wrist, the stiff or medium-stiff rod tip about four inches in an arch. This will cause the bait to shoot upward, naturally. Then, pause a second or two to allow the bait to flutter back to its original spot, keeping in mind that this business portion may be six or eight feet underwater, and it takes a moment for the twitch to be telegraphed downward, and another moment or two for the bait to flutter back. Counting to ten or twelve will help to slow you down. The tendency is to overjig and keep the bait moving so fast a sluggish winter fish can't get at it, even though his belly may be grumbling for your offering. And too violent a jig will frighten many fish away.

Let's suppose you have been jigging properly, and there is still no action. How long is long enough in one zone before moving? The consensus of veteran panfishermen is that fifteen minutes is enough time at one hole, and about five minutes is long enough at any specific depth. Jig, then, for a few minutes in the zone just off the bottom (six to eighteen inches), and raise the bait to where it rests about two feet higher off the bottom. Repeat the jigging there. If the wrist flick just described doesn't work, then maybe it is too violent. Slow down. Vary the twitch.

Of course, when you get a strike, stop. Work this zone. That's the place you should remain until the fish stop hitting or move off. Bobbers have a gadget so that they can be adjusted to hold the bait at different levels. Otherwise, for hand-held rods or handline fishing, markers on the line at certain foot settings will help save time in raising and lowering baits. Your hands, covered with heavy mittens, should be kept warm so that the slight attacks on the bait will not go undetected.

The really good ice fisherman is one who knows how to find fish quickly and then do something about it. His trick is to rig a line with two or more sets of hooks and baits at different levels. One may be at the bottom end of the line, another three or four feet up, and maybe a third or fourth (as the law may permit) on up. Fish this setup until you find where the fish are and on which hook they are taking. Then quickly switch over to the level doing the most business. It is difficult to tie these hooks and rig split shots and bobbers out on the ice. Do this rig preparation at home.

All of these things help locate the fish fast. Visit neighbors on the ice who may be catching fish. Very diplomatically, find out what the bait of the day might be, the levels they are fishing, and any other special tricks.

perch

If the bluegill and his close relatives are king of the panfish in many regions, then surely the common yellow perch *(Perca flavescens)* is the top dog in all other areas and even challenges the sunfishes in their primary range as the most sought-after fish in winter. The perch is popular for many of the same reasons the bluegill and other panfishes are popular—they are not too fussy about the bait they will take and, in general, are fairly easy to catch. They are found just about everywhere, often reach jumbo size (about a pound), and are rated very high for their tasty meat.

Old Yellow Belly is to the young fisherman as the

common cottontail rabbit is to the beginning hunter. And perch are just as widespread and abundant as bunnies. The yellow perch is found over 95 per cent of the ice fishing territory of North America, blanketing the New England and Atlantic states on the east, as far south as the Carolinas, across the Midwest and Great Lakes states, and over the Dakotas, Iowa, Nebraska, and up into all the populated areas of Canada. He is the smallest member of the perch family, although by far the most popular and best known because of his numbers and distribution.

He is one of the most active fish under the ice, because he is one of the most tolerant to low oxygen content and a constant feeder. He is a school fish, even more so than the bluegill. Perch feed on copepods, cladocerans (water fleas), and a variety of plankton early in life. They will also eat insect larvae and scuds, but are not highly selective. As they grow, their tastes change from aquatic insects and their larvae, to crayfish, snails, and a great variety of other fish, including small suckers, sunfish, herring, and sticklebacks. During daylight hours, they feed deep. As it darkens, or on heavy overcast days or under thick ice and a blanket of snow, feeding could be anywhere in the shallowest of waters. They are often caught in a couple of feet or less of water where schools of minnows may be hiding.

Most productive perch bait is a lively minnow about two inches long. He should be hooked with a No. 4 or No. 6 hook just under the top, or dorsal, fin. When starting out, a live minnow is a *must*. After the school moves in, or you move into the school with your rig, a dead minnow can be used to take them, if it is kept moving. Perch sometimes bite so fast and furiously, they can be caught on a cigarette butt, piece of cotton, or a metal spoon with no natural bait on the hook. Small spinners or combination fly and spinner hookups will also fool perch.

Perch activity sometimes is so hot, anglers remove the barbs from their hooks. They raise the hooked fish in a single, sweeping motion, swing him away from the fishing hole, and shake him off the hook into the bucket or onto the ice without ever touching the catch. This allows them to get the lure back where the action is in the shortest possible time. The jigging spoon is probably used more for perch and larger fish than for bluegills and other panfish. Commonly used colors are the fluorescent or fire colors. Yellow is very good. Late in the season, green is found at the end of many a veteran's line. Pearl spoons with red dots are popular. Crappie fishermen seem to favor orange teardrops or tiny spoons with very small minnows attached. In any case, the experts believe the action is more important than the color.

Perch move around more than other panfish because they are always on the prowl for something to eat. Large Northern pike and walleyes are also looking for perch to eat. It is the old story of the little guy being gobbled up by something bigger, so to keep on the move is to keep alive. Like the other panfish, perch will usually be found less than two feet from the bottom. Start there. Use the same techniques of twitching the rod, raising and lowering the bait. The line may be a little heavier; four- to six-pound test is satisfactory.

Bluegill and perch territory overlap a great deal in the same water, so you may hook into a fat perch while trying for other species, and vice versa.

Rigs For Perch. Some anglers tie a three-way swivel on the main line and then two droplines which hang close together. The lines may become twisted, if one of them is hooked to a peppy minnow which swims around. There are many variations of this theme you can play with. Bait and tackle stores are loaded with spreaders, wire hangers, and other rigging paraphernalia. One drawback to the spreader rig: there is some play inherent in the setup which may cause some bites to go undetected. Our rule of thumb is the less junk—knots, swivels, spreaders, flashers, etc.—between the fisherman's hand or bobber and the hook in the fish's mouth, the better off he'll be. Another drawback to complicated rigs: they are cumbersome to manipulate with numb fingers in the teeth of a howling wind.

All of the discussion has been about handlines or lines on small ice rods, but some fishermen like to set out their legal limit of tipups for perch. There is controversy about tipups for perch, because the rig is usually meant for larger fish. Unless the tipup trigger is finely set, an average perch will not be able to trip it. Modern tipups, however, can be set with a light trip, so this old argument won't hold any water. If the law allows enough tipups to make it worthwhile, use them if you like. It isn't practical to rig and tend very many tipups, however, when the action starts. You'd need ice skates to scoot around to take up the catch, rebait, and reset the tipup. It may be better to concentrate attention on working fewer rigs with more finesse than to attempt the scatter-gun approach. After all, there is little sense in using mass production techniques unless they pay off in a larger catch without too much sweat.

crappies

Both black and white crappies make a very respectable name for themselves among ice fishermen over the eastern two thirds of the United States. They are much like blue-gills in size and fighting characteristics and are taken on similar lures, baits, and tackle. As winter drags on, crappie activity drops off until night fishing becomes the best way to take them. One- to one and a half-inch minnows are the best crappie bait, although they will take grubs, larvae, small hunks of liver, pork strips, and raw beef. A few will take streamer flies and small jigs with attractive flutter. Artificials of all kinds don't rate very high here, however.

The crappie feeds mostly on small minnows, and some fishermen feel that the reason more of them are not caught late in the ice fishing season is that they switch to minute crustaceans. Fish with the smallest split shot in your kit and keep the bait at the very end of the line, twitched or fluttered above the fish. The crappie will come up for a bait, but not down on one fished below him.

A white crappie prefers the same general habitat as his brother, but the white crappie can live with dirtier water than the other. Black crappie favor clear lakes or large streams and ponds with some weeds. Best fishing for both species is around weeds. Like the bluegill and most of the panfishes, crappies tend to become stunted because of overpopulation of a body of water. There is a trend across the nation to liberalize or completely remove all size, limit, and season restrictions on stunted fish.

A crappie by any other name might be a calico bass, white bass, speckled bass or speckled perch, or even papermouth or tinmouth.

smelt

The American smelt *(Osmerus mordax)* is a silvery, very delicious fish which reaches a maximum of fourteen inches and weighs a pound or less, and must be considered as a panfish for ice anglers.

Most of the smelt caught with hook and line are taken by ice fishermen with specialized deep-water rigs. Dip netters in the spring take millions upon millions of adult smelt as they migrate up streams to spawn. Smelt, except at spawning time, frequent depths of 40 to 500 feet, but are most often at 60 to 120 feet.

Plankton are the young smelt's first food. He graduates to insect larvae and crustaceans. When smelt reach six inches in size, they begin to feed on tiny fishes and their smaller brother and sister smelt. In the winter, they are feeding almost exclusively on small lake shiners with an occasional sculpin and burbot for a change of pace meal. Smelt also delight in eating *Mysis relicta*, one of the higher crustaceans. *Mysis* is in the class of the crayfish, scud, sow bug, and shrimp which measures a little over an inch in length. We have never heard of ice fishermen using *Mysis* as winter bait. The standard practice is to bait up with a small minnow, about an inch long, lower him to the bottom, and wait.

Smelt move in schools by the thousands, often sticking to the same spots in a big lake or bay year after year. In a few small lakes, they can be fished anywhere from fifteen to sixty feet, but smelt seem to favor the forty-foot mark. To handle this much line, there are two unique rigs in use. One is a bicycle wheel with tire and tube removed. The line is light, two- to four-pound test, and spun on the wheel, which is attached to the inside wall of a fish shanty. When the fish are in, the wheel spins back and forth as the angler hauls up the catch, rebaits the hooks, and runs the line back into the water. This is called "bailing smelt."

The second type of line rack looks like a small wood framework used to dry fish nets. It is nailed or bolted together in a crude octagon outline, about the size of a bicycle wheel, with small pegs to catch and hold the long line. The bicycle wheel, with markers on the line to indicate fish-catching levels, seems to be the most popular and simplest to set up.

A point of caution here. Some states make it illegal to use live smelt for bait, because they don't want this fish introduced into certain lakes. We repeat, there are similar prohibitions regarding goldfish (a member of the carp family) minnows in most states. The smelt hasn't found his rightful place in the fishing world yet. One school of biologists calls him a no-good predator who feeds on the eggs and spawn of young game fish. Another school says he is a good guy, because he is around as food for adult trout, whitefish, herring, and walleyes.

There is no argument, however, among the legions of specialized ice fishermen who spend many pleasant nights in their cozy fish shanties spinning the wheel for smelt from the deep. To these gentlemen, he is a sport fish as well as a mighty good food fish. He is certainly an interesting and tasty pan-size fish for the wintertime angler. In fact he is so good to eat, much of the angler's catch is fried at the fishing shack during the night and never does reach the table back home. It's all part of the frigid fun of panfishing in the winter.

eight

fishing the big ones

Wintertime anglers have always considered trout their most prized under-the-ice catch. "Trout" might mean the kokanee of the West, the lake trout of the Great Lakes region, and the brown and rainbow trout of the Great Lakes and eastern regions.

Big fish of all kinds have a fascination which no pan-fish can match, simply because of the combination of size, eating qualities, and prestige which come with hauling in a lunker.

lake trout

Large reels and six to ten-pound test line are needed in great quantities for lake trout because most fishing is 60 to 100 feet down along the steep dropoffs. Early and late in the ice fishing season, the trout come into more shallow water, but 60 feet is where most lakers are caught.

Hook a six-inch minnow lightly behind the dorsal fin and lower him so that he is about eighteen inches off the bottom. On a second line about fifty feet away, hook a dead herring at the end of the tackle with a split shot pinched on the monofilament line about six feet back. This allows the underwater current to take the herring and enough slack so that if a laker picks it up off the bottom, as often happens, he will swallow it before suspecting anything.

Care must be taken so the live minnow doesn't have enough line to swim down among the logs to hide. The same goes for fishing along or just above weed beds.

Swedish pimples *(Courtesy Michigan Department of Conservation)*

Check the two tipups to make sure the thin crust of ice over the holes does not inhibit the alert flags from springing up into view. Some old-style tipups won't function unless they are absolutely free of ice. Modern traps are rugged for a lifetime of winter fishing, yet delicate enough to be triggered by the slightest bite.

Let us repeat that lake trout are deep rovers. The bait—cut sucker, large minnow or even artificial red or yellow fly, or a Swedish pimple—is fished just a foot to eighteen inches off the bottom. Live bait is best. With artificials or hardware, bobbing (raising and lowering the bait slightly) does the trick. Make it flutter. If you are holding the rod by hand, expect some very soft bites. Trout don't always hammer the bait. Tipups, remember, must be set with light triggers, so the laker can set off the waving flag and get away to swallow the hook. Then the fun begins.

Reel him up or haul him up hand over hand rapidly. Be careful as the fish nears the hole not to bump him under the ice and lose him. He'll fight well deep, ease off once he is tired, and then come to life when he sees the light or the ice fishing hole. The last part of landing a big laker—or a big anything, for that matter—is the most difficult. Nose him up into the hole and grab or gaff him without shaking him off the hook. Once on the ice, wrap the fish in snow, tuck him in a drift, and return to the warm shelter to wait for another big one to take your fresh minnow.

eating habits of fish

Some enterprising biologists in Ontario have done work on the dinner manners of panfish versus big fish.

The Ontario Department of Lands and Forests researchers found that panfish digest 50 per cent of their stomach volume in five hours, 75 per cent in twelve hours, and 100 per cent in twenty-one hours. The digestion time for fish which largely ate insect foods was short. They found that these fish had food in their stomachs at all times of the day and night. This indicates that panfish can be hungry almost any time.

The larger game fish take longer to digest their food. Northern pike, for example, took twenty hours to digest 50 per cent of their stomach contents and fifty hours for 100 per cent. Obviously, when the Northern takes a meal, he settles down to prolonged enjoyment. He won't be hungry all the time. Perhaps this suggests that the angler having trouble finding a hungry Northern pike ought to try panfish! The following is an indication of how much food it takes to keep a fish well fed and prosperous. The amount is surprising. During warm months, bluegills eat 1 to 2 per cent of their body weight per day, according to the Ontario biologists. Three per cent daily is maximum. That is only 0.005 of a pound per day for a quarter-pound bluegill. In other words, the bluegill might eat a pound of invertebrates in the course of a season. Believe it or not, that's a lot of insects. If you don't believe it, try counting a pound of flies!

From a number of different research projects done in New York State and others undertaken by the author, it was found that live suckers, large chubs, and big golden shiners caught more and bigger pike than small or dead baits. Our own survey showed "live bait" was favored about fifteen to one over artificials for all ice fishing. "Live bait" included natural baits such as cut fish flesh, perch eyes, cheese (not natural but something fish could eat), salmon eggs, beef and liver chunks, wigglers, and occasionally worms.

It should be explained that anglers often used the live or natural bait in tandem with a spoon or teardrop ice hook. Did the fish bite because of the attractiveness of the artificial lure, or was it because of the added inducement of the food? Only the fish knows. Like other outdoorsmen, ice fishermen are slow to change from the old, time-tested techniques and baits.

northern pike

This fine game fish is also called jackpike, jack, snake fish, or even pickerel—a name also given to the walleyed pike. Pike *(Esox lucius)*, as we will call him for short, is found throughout Alaska, British Columbia, most sections of eastern Canada, and in almost all of the northern states. He is found also in Iowa, Illinois, and parts of the Ohio Valley, and he has been successfully introduced to many other parts of the United States. Fish biologists love him because of his great appetite and ability to help reduce the number of stunted panfish in many lakes.

Pike generally inhabit shallows, but move into deeper parts of a river or lake to rest. When they are in the shallows, hunting for food and always hungry, they spend much of their time in "pike weeds" and other aquatic weeds. Pike feed heavily very late in the winter just about the same time the ice is getting "rotten" and dangerous to stand on.

That late winter feeding binge may serve to prepare them for spawning in the spring by building up their strength. Around many lakes, cottage development and excessive dredging and filling of the marsh areas have ruined too much pike-spawning territory.

Where adequate spawning grounds are found, the female drops the eggs at random, and several males may accompany her. Pike don't nest like most of the other fish. The young take care of themselves, often turning cannibalistic when small water insects are not abundant. They grow fast and are more than half a foot long at the end of the first season. It takes about three years before the average pike is mature enough to spawn.

Pike of five to ten pounds are common. They often reach ten to thirty pounds in lakes which are not fished hard. The world's record is over fifty pounds.

Not long ago, few fishermen held the Northern pike in very high regard. In fact, some anglers in fish-rich Canadian areas used to kill every pike they "accidentally" caught while fishing for big trout or walleyes. Today, however, with more and more people seeking fish—the bigger the fish the better—pike are being given their due respect.

Give the Northern pike or the chain pickerel a chance to run with the bait. He wants to turn his victim around in his choppers and swallow him head first. You'll know he's doing this, because after the tipup flag begins to wave, the reel will turn as the run begins. It will stop. You haven't lost him. He's just stopping to turn his dinner around for the big swallow. Give him line and give him time. When the reel starts to turn the second time after that important pause, slam the hook home.

The fight on the other end proves he's hooked good. Don't horse. Play the fish, tire him, then bring him up with the same care used for trout. A small gaff should be kept handy for Mr. Pike, unless you are wearing gloves. He's got teeth to spare, and they can cause lacerations if you should try to pull a large pike up through the ice hole by sticking a thumb into his spadelike beak. Use pliers or wear heavy gloves in taking the hook out.

mr. muskellunge

Pike and his large cousin, the muskellunge *(Esox mas-quinongy)*, called the maskinonge in Canada, are often confused. The easiest way to tell them apart is to remember that the pike is dark, usually greyish silver or a shade of green, with light bars or spots. On younger pike there are bars, which break up into light spots in later years.

Muskies are also spotted or barred, but they are dark on a light background. Muskies also are generally larger, and only the upper portions of their cheeks are covered with scales. The pike's cheek is fully covered with scales. Pickerel, by the way, are scale-covered over the entire cheek and gill area. All three have flat, toothy, ducklike snouts and overshot lower jaws.

Esox masquinongy is prized trophy but unfortunately is not plentiful over the ice fishing territory of the United States. He is difficult to catch even in the summer, when he might be in a better mood to strike. Methods and baits for the musky are the same as for Northern pike, only in spades—everything bigger: bigger hooks and bait fish, stronger lines and leaders of wire, longer waits for strikes, and bigger rewards when one does take. This fish has tremendous strength and fighting characteristics, wherever found in its range across southeastern Canada and the Great Lakes and the Mississippi, Tennessee, and St. Lawrence river basins.

Prime musky waters are in the Great Lakes region and Canada. The St. Lawrence has produced some of the largest muskies caught in the last ten years, with the world's record coming from there on September 22, 1957. This fish, weighing 69 pounds, 15 ounces, was caught on hook and line by Arthur Lawton. One fish reported at 102 pounds was caught in Minocqua Lake, Wisconsin, in a net, and several around the 100-pound mark have been found dead on beaches in the Great Lakes area.

Mr. Musky is the lone wolf of big waters. He is solitary and territorial, and when he decides to feed, nothing that swims and no small animal which comes on or near the water is safe. Muskies have been known to eat ducklings, snakes, mice, blackbirds, and other muskies. Primary foods are other fish, often up to several pounds in size. An ice fisherman should offer a large bait. A popular one is a sucker about a foot long. Prepare for a long wait.

Muskies mouth their kill like pike and pickerel. They grab, hold sideways in their hugh mouths, and, after a run, turn the prey and swallow it head first. Use the same care in waiting to set the hook and, if you can hold onto the monster, the same precautions about getting him up through the ice. He is a great and noble fish. Undersize fish should not be injured, so they can be returned to the water to drive another angler to distraction sometime in his future.

If you don't want to keep a fish which has been hooked deep, always cut the leader and return the fish with the hook still in him. Enzymes in the fish will dissolve the hook in a short time, and the critter will survive. Prying out a hook which is deep in a fish usually causes internal injuries which will kill the undersize fish after his return to the water.

chain pickerel

Esox niger is one of the most popular winter fish in the northeastern United States, because he is a ready biter.

In states like Massachusetts, he is undisputed as a prize fish for ice fishermen. He has several common names—the jack or jack fish, the pike, grass pike, and even federation pike because of his chain of thirteen linked rays. He is found from Maine to Florida and in Louisiana, Arkansas, and Tennessee, but very common everywhere east and south of the Allegheny Mountains. He is abundant in the New York lakes. Because of their small size, grass pickerel and redfin pickerel, close relatives of the chain pickerel, attract little attention from fishermen. The chain averages only a couple of pounds, but occasionally will reach five pounds.

Best winter baits are small minnows on or near the bottom in shallow water around weeds. Pickerel will, however, eat almost anything that moves, any time. Generally, the smaller the fish, the closer to shore he will be. Larger fish like slightly deeper water, except in the late winter, when they prowl the shallows looking for spawning sites. To illustrate the voracity of the chain pickerel's appetite, two young five-inch pickerel were put in a trough with a large school of one-inch minnows. The two pickerel ate 128 minnows the first day, 132 the second, and 150 the third, and they increased about one inch in length in 48 hours! Vicious little devils! They feed day and night, year round, mostly early in the morning or late in the evening, the best times to fish. Like his big cousin, the Northern pike, the pickerel ambushes most of its prey, seizing it crosswise in its toothy jaws. As the victim struggles, the pickerel swims slowly away, and with somewhat jerky movements, it maneuvers the prey until it is headfirst in the mouth. Ingestion proceeds with another series of jerky motions.

Speed of ingestion depends on the relative size of the predator to its prey. Ice fishermen, then, should let the chain pickerel, like the Northern pike, take the bait and run with it, and give it time to swallow. There will be times when the fish will hook himself immediately, but best let it have its run as the reel turns freely. If the fish feels resistance, he may spit out the bait and beat it.

The chain pickerel is true to the pike family of fishes in that it is solitary in behavior, exhibiting no schooling tendencies. Larger fish tend to move into shallow water at night and back to deeper water during the day. The more overcast it is, the better for fishing, because they seem to linger in the shallows and remain active. There is a large turnover, a heavy mortality from angling and natural causes, with the average longevity three to four years. Utilization through angler-harvest, then, seems like good conservation, since the fish cannot be stockpiled. As with so many of the other warm-water fishes, pickerel management means catching your fish and helping the remaining ones by taking some pressure off the habitat.

There has been a long-standing controversy on the effects of ice fishing on pickerel populations. It is widely held in the New England states that winter anglers are more effective than summer fishermen. In certain Connecticut lakes, ice fishermen harvested over 40 per cent of the total annual catch, although summer anglers were six and a half times more plentiful. Similar figures are available for New Jersey and Massachusetts. In addition, it is possible that ice fishing may in some regions at some times take more females than males. Some biologists feel this is due to the need for the female to fatten up prior to the early spring breeding season. In view of all this, there have been limitations on the number of fish, length of the ice fishing season, and the minimum size, but through it all, fish experts have found ice fishing really has little effect on year-to-year pickerel populations. They call it poor management not to harvest the fish which would be lost through natural mortality before the next summer. New England chain pickerel fishing is not much different from lake trout fishing.

walleye

No matter what we call this bug-eyed fish—walleye, pike, perch, yellow pike, etc.—the walleye (*Stizostedion vitreum*) loves to eat large quantities of minnows summer or winter, and fishermen love to eat large quantities of walleyes. He is the darling of fishermen from Alabama to Hudson's Bay, Canada. He is found in the winter in deep water, fifteen to thirty feet or more, over reefs, on the edges of shoals where water is moving, and where springs or streams enter frozen lakes. Walleyes, moving in schools, always seem to be on the prowl for minnows, which make up over 90 per cent of their diet.

In open-water fishing, the dedicated walleye man waits until evening or complete darkness before starting to fish, since the walleye is a nocturnal feeder. In the winter, however, these nocturnal habits are not so pronounced, because ice and snow blot out the daylight. Overcast, windy days are still best in winter walleye angling. These fish, which are prize catches in Minnesota, Wisconsin, Ontario, Quebec, Michigan, and throughout most of north central America, move toward shore at night, summer or winter, to hunt minnows. They also seek out the springs and streams mentioned above, as well as cracks or openings in the ice where the oxygen content is higher. Late winter fishing drops off fast. January and February are best. March sees a big reduction in the catch of walleyes, and April is very dull fishing. It could be that the spring spawning dampens the usually voracious appetite for minnows. Some speculate that the walleye may shift to another food in this period just before spawning, and this is why ice fishermen don't catch them.

Walleyes usually don't weigh much over three pounds, although many which run ten to fifteen pounds are taken in the more remote lakes of the Great Lakes states and Canada. The world's record is around twenty-four pounds. Since the average walleye is but a few pounds, six-pound test line is most often used through the ice with small (No. 2) hooks in very lively minnows. Tipups are preferred over handlines, although a handline is more practical when the school comes to life and action is fast. When bait is short, a dead minnow jigged actively occasionally works. Silver spoons and Swedish jigs weighing one-eighth to three-fourths of an ounce with a dead minnow impaled crosswise on the hooks are popular.

There usually isn't much doubt about a walleye strike. They are one of the hardest biters under the ice, normally hooking themselves when they clamp down on the bait or jig.

sauger

The sauger (Stizostedion canadense) is so much like the walleye, few fishermen realize the difference. Sauger has large, odd, dark body blotches and rows of dark spots. The walleye has a single black blotch at the back of the dorsal fin. Sauger are usually smaller, averaging a pound, with some extra big ones reaching three to five pounds. Biologists report some anglers catching seven- and eight-pound saugers actually have a hybrid cross between a sauger and a walleye. The range of this fish is more westward than the walleye. In Wyoming and Montana, it can be caught in open water year round.

Ice fishing tactics for sauger are much the same as for walleyes, except that smaller minnows and smaller hooks are in order. Sauger like clear, deep streams and lakes with sand bottoms. They also like the darkness of night and overcast days.

whitefish

Less important than the sauger on the list of "big ones" of ice fishing are the whitefish of New England, eastern Canada, and the Great Lakes. They are fine fish for eating, but restricted in their distribution. Whitefish are spear-men's targets in some lakes, but the spearfishing usually is done from boats with underwater lights and not enough through the ice to be worth more than a mention here for the record.

The whitefish are restricted, because they need large, deep, cold lakes, where they are found rather regularly fifty feet or deeper. They are bottom-feeding and school fish which feed on small minnows, crustaceans and some vegetable matter. Small minnows are the best bait for the delicate mouths of these fish. Inexperienced fisher-men lose many whitefish before they realize they are tearing the hooks out of their mouths. Chopped bait, diced liver, and bacon scraps are sometimes used as chum, but it is not required.

Dacron lines are used by some oldtimers who claim

there is too much stretch in even the best, most modern monofilament line in depths over 50 to 100 feet. They like the old, stiff line to set the hook quickly—a necessary thing with timid biters like these.

Lake whitefish *(Coregonus clupeaformis)* were highly prized by commercial netters in the Great Lakes before parasitic sea lamprey nearly wiped them out along with most of the lake trout in Huron, Superior, and Lake Michigan. Today the lake trout and whitefish are coming back and gaining in popularity with sport fishermen. Cisco, round whitefish, and mountain whitefish are also taken occasionally through the ice of Canada and the northwestern United States. None is exceptional as a game fish. They do not put up a fight like any of the trouts, but they are delicious eating fish and difficult to land because of their soft, almost toothless mouths.

Whether your big fish is a kokanee you're trying to snag in Colorado's Granby or Shadow Mountain reservoirs or a giant lake trout, there is a fascinating and unexplainable thrill to hooking into a really big fish.

nine

spearing through the ice

Spear fishing, one of the oldest forms of fishing done by man, is also one of the most controversial, because it is so deadly.

Those opposed to spearing claim there is little or no sport involved, that it is brutal and too effective. They say that many sublegal-size fish are destroyed by inexperienced spearmen. A nineteen-inch Northern pike, speared in a state where twenty inches is the minimum size, has little chance of surviving with two or three spear holes in his back, the critics point out.

the sportsmanship of spear fishing

Actually, refraction makes fish appear smaller than they are. Dedicated spearmen answer that they can tell the difference between a legal and a nonlegal fish before they let go of the weapon, but they often pass up a legal fish, • because refraction fools even the best of them. Under water, one foot appears to be about nine inches.

To the charge that spearing is brutal and bloodthirsty, the spearmen answer that it is no more brutal than hook-and-line fishing. The warm weather fisherman rarely sees blood, and for some mysterious reason, he thinks his is a gentle art, but his fish die just as dead as the ones speared. And it is no more bloodthirsty than bow-and-arrow deer hunting, or bowfishing for rough fish in the spring. Anyone who says spearing is not sporting, just hasn't tried it himself.

The basic difference between spearing and hook-and-line fishing is that in the former, the fish really doesn't have to decide to go all the way after a decoy, as in the latter. In hook-and-line fishing, the fish sees a lure or bait. Or he smells it in the water. Then he decides if he is angry enough or hungry enough to take a swipe at it. If he does, and he gets hooked, then it is his own fault.

In spearing, the fish sees a decoy in the water and comes after it. If the spearman is on his toes, he might get a split second to fire his weapon at the fish. In short, spearing is more like hunting than true angling.

The typical spearman in North America is a pike hunter. He needs a fairly large hole, anywhere from two by three to three by four feet in size. He also needs a light-proof tent or spearing shanty so he can see his target in the water.

decoys

Although a pike or a musky will eat just about anything that won't eat him first—and this includes such odd fare as snakes, frogs, blackbirds, mice, young ducks, crayfish, and other pike and muskies—a large shiner is the best spearing decoy. Large suckers are also good, because they live longer on a string, but the number one decoy seems to be the shiner.

To add to the decoy's lifetime, it should be carefully strung on a fine wire which is inserted just under the top fin but not through the vital spinal cord. This wire is then bent around and tied to the stout line. Properly attached, a good golden shiner or sucker may last through an entire season for the spearman. They cost anywhere from two for a quarter to a dollar each, depending on the area and demand.

Recently, spearmen have been using plastic or wooden decoys with some success. They are weighted and designed so that they remain upright, and with a little twitch of the line from above, they appear to move. There are some the modern ice fishermen use today which are battery-powered, so that they "swim" in the water.

The oldtimers prefer the healthy, active, live decoy who is also a watchdog under the ice. It is not that he so much wants to help you, but he does know when danger (a pike or musky) is near, and he wants to save his own skin. A healthy decoy becomes nervous and active when a big fish comes within range. He will fight the restraining line, swim up under the ice, and even try to come back up through the hole to escape the one who wants to make a meal of him.

Pike may come into view at any level. Bigger ones seem to prefer the very bottom, but don't count on it. There are times when several pike will move in at once, eyeing the decoy without attempting to kill it. To say the least, they are unpredictable.

Typical behavior—if there is such a thing for a pike—is to move in, circle a little, and then smash the decoy with his powerful jaws when it is broadside. The kill may come a moment or two after the decoy relaxes, apparently feeling secure that the pike is not going to strike. This may be what actually triggers the pike into action.

Non-typical behavior is for a pike to come into view and then lie there for maybe twenty or thirty minutes just watching the decoy. It is maddening to have this happen with a trophy-size pike just out of range.

Occasionally several smaller pike, called hammerhandles move in together like a band of toughies traveling in a pack. The spearman should frighten them off with his spear before they slash his decoy to pieces. If he tries to raise the decoy from the water, it may only provoke a gang attack. Pike, often nervy critters, may follow a decoy up out of the water so far that their entire heads are inside the spearman's shanty, but this is unusual.

Pike are wanderers, although they prefer weedy areas, as stated. They do have more or less regular routes of travel through heavy weeds, and the smart ice fisherman knows how to spot these. Using the spy-hole method described in the chapter "let's go fishing," a spearman can spot channels through weed beds or natural valleys in the lake bottom where big fish prowl. Bait fish hide in these weeds, and the pike knows this. He also knows his chances for a kill in thick weeds are slim so he sticks to the relatively open areas or "paths" between the weeds.

Some fishermen go so far as to say the pike travels specific routes as foxes do in hunting field mice and other foods.

"Shallow" water for a pike may be anything from just a couple feet of water to six or eight feet. In the deeper water, it is very important to prime the bottom with corn, beans, and other items mentioned earlier in the chapter "let's go fishing."

Bottom priming in this case is to reflect light and not so much to lure fish. Tinfoil is a good reflector for this.

spearing techniques

The best practice is to have the sharp, barbed prongs of the spear in the water before a pike shows himself. Of course, it is impossible to hold such a spear poised for a long time, so try this: Use a battery clamp or heavy-duty clothespin to clip the spear rope to the shanty ceiling. This should be rigged so that when the spearman wants to move into action, the clip or pin will easily come unfastened.

There is less splash this way when the spear thrust is made, and less noise to frighten the target.

But another bugaboo comes into the picture, namely, refraction, that quirk of physics which makes a straight line appear to bend under the surface of water. In other words, the pike isn't where he seems to be. Only experience can teach one how much allowance to make for this. It is like knowing how much to lead a fast-flying duck with a shotgun blast.

In short, the spear should be thrust under and a little

ahead of the target. Aiming a little ahead gives you a little lead to compensate for that split-second burst of speed the fish will make when he senses he is under attack. Aiming a little under takes care of the refraction factor. The deeper the water, the more allowance should be made for both factors.

There is no real concern for refraction if the fish is directly below. Shoot for the back of the head, the most vital spot.

An average pike or musky spear is an all-steel affair about five or six feet long with at least three and preferably five or six prongs.

The smart spearman never tries to lift a fish out of the water immediately. If a hit is made, he lets the spear go, so that the fish will spend himself without wiggling free. In water shallow enough, the impaled fish is held against the bottom, so that he cannot flip free. Remember, pike are amazingly hard to kill. It is common for one to "come back to life" when he is lifted into a shanty and has a chance to slash at the fisherman with his teeth or knock over a heater with his powerful, slender body. They should not be considered landed until they are rolled and packed in snow out on the ice.

Be advised to have all things fastened down in the shanty and the door open to get away from the hole fast.

Working in deep water, some spearmen tie the rope to the head of the weapon to permit lifting the pike prongs first and to help prevent him from slipping free. This system is debatable, because the rope tied to the spear head causes extra disturbance in the water as it is thrown.

A rope at the spearhead also affects the planing angle

of the weapon and may cause a miss. The other end of the rope should be tied securely to the shanty with enough coiled rope out free where it can be fed out as the spear is thrown. This is especially important when after the giant sturgeon and very big pike and muskies.

the importance of dark and quiet

Sometimes pike are more spooky and nervous because of bright light. This could be sunlight or light in the shanty. There isn't much that can be done about the sun except to pile snow around the shanty to cut down some of the light and seal the spearman against the elements at the same time. Of course, the shanty should be as light-tight as a photographer's darkroom.

Pike have been known to beat it at the slightest movement of the man in the shanty above. The very serious put on dark leather gloves which serve a dual purpose. They reflect less light, glowing up from the lake bottom, and give the spearman a better grip on the cold steel spear handle.

Overcast or clear, the bigger the pike, the more difficult they are to spear. They don't grow large by being stupid.

A pike will disappear in a flash at the slightest noise from boots on the shanty floor or a passing car on the ice or other sounds which cause vibrations to pass through the water. Talking in a normal conversational voice does not seem to disturb fish but the quieter the better. Small radios playing softly do no harm. In fact, some of the new transistors, turned up very loud, will even attract some fish. This is done by putting the ear plug into the water and letting the music flow. There has been no research yet on whether ear-shattering aspirin commercials frighten fish.

For the most part, however, the serious spearman must learn to sit as quietly and as patiently as a hunter on a deer runway waiting for a big buck.

novelty spearing

All spearing isn't done inside a shanty. There is a novel method of spearing fish which involves driving the fish with beaters much the same way as deer and other game are driven toward waiting guns.

This is done on some frozen rivers or in narrow bays of lakes where a trench can be cut in the ice from one shore to the other.

The slit is several feet wide and lined with one team of spearmen about a spear's length apart. The second team, the beaters, move several hundred yards upstream, in a river, or back on the shore on a bay.

The beaters, walking very slowly, bang their ice spuds or large clubs on the ice and advance toward the waiting spearmen.

The noise drives the fish toward the open trench, where the action is furious. At times, the bottom is black with fish.

But just as in a deer drive, this method has its own dangers. The biggest danger is breaking through along the open trench. Ice cut all the way across is very dangerous.

Critics of this technique claim it is slaughter and not sport, but it is no more slaughter than a deer drive, in which the animals are panicked toward waiting rifles.

It serves a good purpose in ridding certain waters of carp, suckers, and other so-called trash fish.

Traditional spearing, however, is for the great Northern pike or the muskellunge. But there are some other good targets, such as dogfish and gar, besides the trash fish mentioned just above.

the sturgeon

Giant sturgeon are the largest fish taken by ice fishermen, but their range is restricted to the Pacific Northwest and the upper midsection of the United States and Canada. The white sturgeon is the one found in the West from California to Alaska, while the lake sturgeon is king in mid-America and Canada. The home waters of the prehistoric-looking shovelnose sturgeon are in Mississippi and Alabama, where there is little or no ice fishing, but he does reach up into the Missouri River to Montana, a section where winter fishing is catching on big.

Catching a sturgeon on a hook-and-line is largely a matter of luck—more so than in any other type of real angling. They suck their food up from the bottom and don't readily take a baited hook.

In sections like northern Michigan's Burt and Mullett lakes, sturgeon are a big attraction where spearing is the most productive way to catch them. To see one over a hundred pounds here is not unusual.

The technique is the same as for large pike and muskies, except that everything is magnified—the decoy, the spear, the wait, and the thrill. Two a year is the Michigan limit for these monsters, who have been known to pull many a grown spearman into the drink.

Successfully landing one just about guarantees many,

Spearing a sturgeon like this is a lifetime thrill. This one taken in Michigan was over six feet long. (*Courtesy Michigan Department of Conservation*)

many excellent meals, besides getting your picture in the paper.

There have been many wild, unbelievable stories about sturgeon seven or eight feet long knocking a spear-man cold and wrecking a shanty with his powerful hulk. Rugged sport, it certainly is.

This brings us back to the original question here: Is spearing sport?

Answer that for yourself after trying it just once.

ten

conservation and sportsmanship

There is a heap of scientific data from Massachusetts to Montana and points in between that shows winter fishing is more productive per hour than summer or open-water angling.

Fisheries biologists Warren Churchill and Howard Snow in Wisconsin found that over half (55 per cent) of the time spent fishing (angler days) occurred during the summer period. Spring fishing accounted for 26 per cent of the angling activity, fall fishing, 5 per cent, and winter or ice fishing, 14 per cent. And in the same survey, Churchill and Snow discovered that of all the fish caught, 20 per cent were taken in the winter, 27 per cent in the spring, 49 per cent in the summer, and only 4 per cent in the fall. In part of their study dealing with the Murphy Flowage, they found the winter catch was disproportionately high, 32 per cent, and they said this was because of the abundant bluegills readily caught through the ice. At Murphy Flowage, the biologists found bluegills supplied the bulk of fishing during all seasons, yet they were caught more than twice as fast in winter as in summer! On Wisconsin's Escanaba Lake, perch and walleyes are the principal species in the winter catch, and on the average the harvest of these was about 61 per cent higher in winter than in summer. Of course in some months and in some years during the test, fishing was absolutely fantastic. Snow and Churchill reported that some anglers averaged one bluegill for each minute of fishing time. The 1960 average, however, was about 8.1 fish per hour in the winter.

The Wisconsin biologists said, "Ice fishermen as a group differ in several ways from summer anglers. They are fewer in number but better fishermen since cold weather discourages 'amateurs' and the half-hearted. They are usually local residents who know the lakes they are fishing. As a result, they are likely to enjoy better success in the capture of those species that bite in winter.

"Where the fish population of a lake is made up largely of species that bite in winter, the composition of the catch is predominantly the same all year. However, since these fish bite faster in winter, the average number of fish caught per trip is greater during this season. Such is the case at Murphy Flowage where the predominant species are bluegill, perch, crappies and Northern pike. Here the average catch per trip is 13½ in winter compared to seven in summer."

Biologists in Michigan came up with more supporting testimony that winter fishing for species which bite under the ice is far more productive per man-hours of angling than summer angling for these same species.

Michigan's studies, done by the Institute of Fisheries Research, also indicated summer fishing does not suffer from the toll taken during the winter by ice fishermen. Here were some of the findings:

1. Ice fishermen didn't fish as long each day, but had greater catches per hour.

2. Summer anglers took more fish per man, because they fished longer each time out.

3. The catch per hour during the winter months was 1.7 fish, or about twice that of the summer months, when anglers caught 0.9 fish per hour.

4. Because of deep snows during the study (before the popularity of snowmobiles), winter anglers tended to concentrate their attention on lakes near roads, whereas summer fishermen with no weather restrictions on their travel spread out more.

It should be pointed out that the Michigan studies mentioned were primarily concerned with southern panfish lakes which received a lot of attention from a cross section of anglers, while the Wisconsin study reported earlier was on northern lakes where natives were the primary anglers.

A Massachusetts study of winter fishing found that restrictions on fishermen "will have little or no effect on the quality of future fishing. The past history of fisheries management was characterized by such approaches." Biologist James Mullan wrote: "Most notably, many waters were closed in the past to winter ice fishing for a number of years and when finally re-opened, they failed miserably to live up to expectations. The future of fishing appears to depend primarily on the detection and control of environmental factors such as over-crowding by small panfishes rather than on greatly limiting the take by anglers . . ."

In all the research projects studied, it was clear that fish, like wild game, cannot be stockpiled. There is a great annual turnover in wildlife and fish populations which must be harvested or lost to nature. A body of water can support just so many fish and no more, the scientists said. The harvest by ice fishermen is insignificant compared to the fish lost from shoreline destruction and water pollution each year.

In answer to the once common charge that ice anglers were "meat hunters," New Jersey biologist Roland F. Smith answered some of the common questions in a report he titled "Fact and Fable About Ice Fishing and Ice Fishermen." Here are some of the more interesting questions and answers. (Keep in mind pickerel are the primary fish here.)

Q: *Are more females than males caught through the ice?*

A: This concept is essentially false. Studies on the sex ratio of pickerel caught from our major north Jersey lakes during an entire ice season will generally reveal a ratio that comes as close to fifty-fifty as one could expect.

Q: *Do ice fishermen catch more fish than open-water anglers?*

A: This is a widely accepted belief, and one that is supported by scientific evidence. A comparison of the average number of "take-home" fish caught by pickerel fishermen throughout the year shows that the ice fisherman is very definitely the most successful, followed by the spring fisherman, then the fall and finally the summer angler. [These are roughly the same ratios found for spring, summer, and fall anglers in a Wisconsin study. Remember the New Jersey study dealt with pickerel almost exclusively, and pickerel are the primary winter fish in this eastern state.]

Q: *Are more large pickerel caught during ice season than during open-water season?*

A: This notion would appear to have considerable basis in fact since the former world's record from Green Pond and the present one from Massachusetts were both taken through the ice. More large pickerel would be caught in the summer, but anglers don't fish down deep where the big ones like to linger.

Q: *Do fish bite best during ice season?*

A: This is not as widely accepted in all quarters, for there are many who will insist that pickerel can be more readily caught in the early spring. Just because ice fishermen harvest more pickerel does not necessarily mean that the pickerel bite best at that time of year. After all, the average ice angler will use about 6½ tipups, as compared to the open-water angler who will fish with about 1¼ rods. One way to check this assumption is to employ the same standard of measurement for each type of fishing; i.e., the fishing line, fishing for a given period of time. On this basis [pickerel in New Jersey], it seems fishing during the winter is perhaps the least efficient of all in terms of the number of fish that are caught per average line-hour. It is immediately realized, then, that it is the number of lines employed, not the caliber of fishing, or availability of fish, that gives the ice fishermen the edge.

Q: *Is it true ice fishing is detrimental to open-water fishing?*

A: This statement, as such, is generally false. Massachusetts closed certain lakes to all ice fishing for as long as three years to try to answer this question. [The Massachusetts lake closings proved a "miserable failure."] Thus, it is indicated that ice fishing allows for the harvest of fish that would otherwise not be taken by anyone. Properly regulated then, ice fishing should help provide for a maximum harvest of pickerel at any given lake without reducing that population to the point where the open-water fishing is made worse . . . One thing for certain—ice fishing must be considered as an integral part of the sport-fishing picture. It must be given fair consideration in any fisheries management program. Perhaps, in the future, ice fishermen may even be looked upon as true conservationists in the sense that they can be counted upon to play an important role in harvesting a segment of the pickerel population that otherwise would never be taken.

Ice fishermen who have been at it more years than they like to remember know winter fishing is good and that is probably the main reason they are out there. They also know there are many intangibles about ice fishing that can't really be measured. They know there is a certain magic in walking on water—frozen water, of course. They just like being outdoors and watching the geese honk south in the fall when new ice forms, and honk north in the spring when the ice becomes mushy underfoot.

They're a special breed, but share the outdoorsman's love and appreciation of wild things and nature—even frosty, blue-white, ice-cold nature. They get just as angry with the litterbugs who throw beer cans, paper, cartons, and other trash on the ice. Like all good sportsmen, they detest the miscreant who trespasses on private property or cuts limbs off a cottage owner's private tree for firewood and gives all fishermen a bad image.

Maybe they are a bunch of unusual coconuts, and maybe they don't look so pretty waddling around in their heavy clothes like spacemen, but they like it that way. They look at ice fishing as good sport, a growing sport. Come on out and punch a hole in the ice for yourself sometime.

eleven

ice fishing in different regions

There are more than six million ice fishermen in the United States and Canada scattered from Nova Scotia to Alaska and from the Arctic to—believe it or not—Arizona! Heaviest concentrations of frigid fishermen are in the Midwest, Ohio, Pennsylvania, New York, New England, Ontario, and Quebec.

In order to get the most complete picture of ice fishing in all of North America, we contacted fishing experts in all the ice fishing states, 34 of them, and all the Canadian provinces for information. We wanted to get some of the local or regional techniques, state and provincial rules and regulations, and some tips on consistent hot spots. Because there are always minor year-to-year changes in laws pertaining to fishermen and fishing, we have not attempted to give a detailed rundown on all the regulations. We have, however, included enough information so that a man in New York, for example, might know when the best time to fish in Pennsylvania or Illinois might be. We have also included the addresses of the fish and conservation departments, so a reader can write direct for the latest tips and regulations.

THE UNITED STATES

ALASKA—Department of Fish and Game, Subport Building, Juneau

Fishing is a year round proposition in Alaska, with some exceptions for specified closed waters listed in the Fish and Game Department regulations. Northern pike and whitefish may be speared in certain waters.

Rainbow trout, silver salmon, Northern pike, and burbot, in this order, are Alaska's most sought-after winter fish. Some Alaskans use small canned shrimp and salmon eggs for bait, because the use of live fish is prohibited in fresh waters here. The important lakes, out of all the thousands in Alaska, are Finger Lake and Echo Lake near Palmer; Jan and Lisa lakes near Fairbanks; and Salmon Creek Reservoir near Juneau.

Eskimo ice fishermen of today are using more commercially manufactured lures and lines. The hand-carved ivory lures and lines fabricated from animal material are still common items with Eskimos who catch sheefish, Northern pike, whitefish, trout, char, and burbot through the ice. Coastal Eskimos take flounder, cod, sheefish, whitefish, burbot, char, and king crab. Eskimos make most catches by jigging, but some bait fishing is still done.

ARIZONA—Game and Fish Department, 120 Arizona State Building, 1688 W. Adams, Phoenix

Arizona, land of deserts, painted mountains, and spectacular warm, dry weather, has some excellent ice fishing, believe it or not. The Fort Apache Indian Reservation, with its controversial man-made reservoirs, has been developing fishing areas rapidly in recent years. Another popular ice fishing area is the Nelson Reservoir near Springerville. There are some other lakes which occasionally have good ice fishing. These include Luna Lake, near Alpine, and some of the lakes in the Show Low-Lakeside-Pinetop area. Others which get special mention include Ashurst, Kinnichinick, Big and Lee Valley lakes. Remember these are considerable distances from major highways and may be inaccessible because of winter road conditions. The ice buggies, snowmobiles, and motorized toboggans come into play here.

CALIFORNIA—Department of Fish and Game, Resources Building, 1416 Ninth St., Sacramento

California is the newest state to join the ranks of those with legalized winter ice-fishing. The green light was given on January 1, 1969 when angling through the ice was authorized at a few designated waters where year-around angling was already allowed. The regulations were later changed to permit year-around trout angling at most lakes in the state. In the colder mountain regions, where waters freeze, this meant ice fishing.

Davis Lake, located in the Plumas National Forest near the city of Portola on highway #70, is by far the most heavily used water. This popularity is explained by a large population of rainbow trout, and the fact that the road leading to the lake is paved and kept open during the winter months.

The portion of the reservoir which lies a few hundred yards out from the rockfill dam receives the greatest angling pressure. On a balmy winter weekend from 100 to 200 hopefuls can be observed on the ice—a crowd by California ice fishing standards. More adventuresome anglers use snowmobiles to travel to the more remote corners of the reservoir.

Trout are the big draw at most ice fishing waters, although some lakes offer largemouth bass and bluegill. Other Golden State lakes which have found favor with ice fishing addicts include Antelope, Dorris, Stampede and Prosser Reservoirs. Visitor use at these waters is often limited because of poor accessibility. Numerous other lakes in the mountain country freeze over during the winter months, but are seldom fished because they then are not easily reached.

California ice fishermen are rather unsophisticated when compared to those in the Midwestern states. Ice shanties have yet to appear. Tip-ups are not used because of a regulation which limits each angler to a single, closely attended line. Bait fishing is the most popular technique. Salmon eggs are the favorite. Yet some of the largest trout landed by Golden State anglers have been taken by persons jigging with Swedish Pimple lures. Jigs are also extremely effective on largemouth bass.

COLORADO—State Department of Game, Fish and Parks, 6060 Broadway, Denver

Colorado fishing is year round for all species, except during the spawning closures listed in the state fishing regulations. Unusual in ice fishing is the kokanee salmon snagging, which is widespread in Colorado. This starts in November and continues through December. Fishermen then turn to whitefish in January and yellow perch late in this month. Perch fishing is usually good until early March, and trout fishing is good here when the ice is at least four inches thick on lakes and reservoirs.

Colorado ice fishermen like live minnows (where permitted), salmon eggs, cheese, and spleen. Best lakes for trout are Lake John, Vaga Reservoir, and Eleven Mile Reservoir. Best warm-water lakes are Boyd, Bonny, Jackson, and Jumbo Reservoir. Most of Colorado's 50,000 ice fishermen hit these spots and spend nearly half a million dollars annually on their sport.

Kokanee snagging areas include Granby and Shadow Mountain reservoirs and Grand Lake, Grand County. Good snagging starts around November 25 each winter. Taylor Reservoir, Gunnison County; Vallecito Reservoir, La Plata County; and Skaguay Reservoir, Fremont County, are also good at this time. Carter and Horsetooth reservoirs won't generally produce good snagging until after mid-December.

CONNECTICUT—Board of Fisheries and Game, State Office Building, Hartford

Connecticut has more than a quarter of a million fishermen, and, according to the Sport Fishing Institute, approximately one-third of them go ice fishing. Pickerel, perch, and black crappie are the three prime winter fishes. Best fishing is in the western part of the state in Lake Lillionanah, Bangam Lake, and East Twin Lake.

There is no closed season, except in specified lakes, for panfish. Techniques used here are along typical lines.

DELAWARE—Board of Fish and Game Commissioners, Dover

Ice fishing is very restricted in Delaware because of the marginal ice conditions. Ice fishing lasts only a few days a year, most winters, because of safety factors.

IDAHO—Fish and Game Department, 518 Front St., Boise

Idaho is another state where ice fishing is just emerging as a major winter sport. Major ice fishing target is whitefish. Rules for winter fishing are simple, since most of the ice fishing is done on a few lakes. The better spots are Pend Oreille Lake in northern Idaho, Payette Lake in the central area at McCall, Idaho, and the Payette River north of Boise, when the weather is cold enough to freeze the stream.

ILLINOIS—Conservation Department, State Office Building, 400 South Spring St., Springfield

The Illinois Conservation Department reported that this big ice fishing state is famous for its bluegill and crappie angling through the ice, a sport enjoyed by nearly 200,000 winter anglers.

Illinois laws stipulate that shelters must not be left unattended or overnight on the ice after March 1 each season. This is a safety measure. Tipups cannot be left unattended at any time. The season is from mid-December until mid-March, depending, of course, on weather conditions.

Illinois anglers favor the Fox Chain O' Lakes just northwest of Chicago. These include Challe Lake, Catherine Lake, Lake Marie, Grass Lake, Fox Lake, and Pistakee Lake. Crab Orchard Lake in the south and many of the Mississippi and Illinois River backwaters are excellent producers too. Farm ponds, strip mine lakes, and gravel pits are favored by many who also hit the artificial lakes hard.

INDIANA—Conservation Department, 605 State Office Building, Indianapolis

Indiana ranks with Michigan, Illinois, New York, Ohio, Wisconsin, Minnesota, and a few other major ice fishing states, with well over 150,000 ice anglers. There are large creel limits or none at all on popular species including bluegills, crappies, rock bass, large and smallmouth bass, pike, perch, catfish, and roughfish.

There are many popular lakes in Indiana, mostly in the northern and central areas in the natural lake region. Besides the natural lakes, there are many farm ponds, reservoirs, gravel pits, and other artificial lakes.

Indiana's handy little *Sportsman's Guide* booklet neatly lists the public access sites and gives the liberal regulations clearly and simply.

IOWA—State Conservation Commission, East 7th & Court Ave., Des Moines

Ice fishermen using shanties must obtain a Conservation Commission permit before going fishing.

Regular season rules and regulations apply to ice fishermen, with some exceptions noted in the Commission's pamphlet of laws. Perch lead the parade of popular winter fish, with bluegills and walleyes close behind. The most publicized ice fishing areas are along the Mississippi from Guttenburg north to the border and, second, the lakes area in Dickinson, Palo Alto, and Emmett counties. Farm ponds in the south and southeastern regions are third in popularity.

KANSAS—Forestry, Fish and Game Commission, Box F, Pratt

Due to weather conditions, ice fishing in Kansas is extremely limited, with few involved in the sport. Kansas does have ultraliberal regulations, however. They say simply "no closed season on any species of fish" and "no size limit on any species." There are daily creel limits, but they are ultraliberal also.

MAINE—Department of Inland Fisheries and Game, State House, Augusta

Salmon, lake trout, pickerel, perch, and smelt, in this order, are Maine's primary winter fish. The Department of Inland Fisheries and Game offers a 23-page booklet with all the ice fishing laws given by counties.

Most popular ice fishing lake is Moosehead Lake in the Belgrade region. There are also many other good lakes.

MASSACHUSETTS—Department of Natural Resources, 73 Tremont St., Boston

Prime winter fish here are chain pickerel (*Esox niger*) and yellow perch. Of lesser importance, with possibly a few local exceptions, are largemouth and smallmouth bass, white perch, the trouts, walleye, and Northern pike.

Bait fish are prohibited on reclaimed trout ponds. Most Bay State ice fishermen use tipups baited with a shiner, jigging spoon, or lure. Jigging lures are frequently baited with the usual salmon eggs and worms. The perch eye is especially popular in Massachusetts.

MICHIGAN—State Conservation Department, Stevens T. Mason Building, Lansing

Michigan is undisputed king of all the ice fishing states, with around half a million ice fishermen. The department publishes a list of specially designated lakes where it is legal to ice fish for rainbow and brown trout in January and February. In addition, Michigan is probably the leading state for spear fishing. Northern pike are the most important target for spearmen.

Bluegills, perch, crappie, Northern pike, and walleyes —in that order—are the most important winter fish. To encourage ice fishing, dozens of Michigan communities annually conduct fish festivals and carnivals on the frozen lakes. The largest such festival in the country is called "Tipup Town, U.S.A.," and is held each January at Houghton Lake, Michigan's largest inland lake.

Other popular areas are Saginaw Bay, Lake St. Clair near Detroit, and the lakes in the northern section of the lower peninsula.

Lampreys, live carp, and goldfish are not permitted as baits, for obvious reasons. There are special brochures available from the Michigan Tourist Council in Lansing or the Conservation Department for non-residents who want to learn more about Michigan fishing opportunities. All material, as in other states, is available free on request.

MINNESOTA—Conservation Department, St. Paul

The big attraction for Minnesota anglers is the walleye, which comes in large economy sizes. The state also has a wide variety of other prime fish, but the walleye is given as the most important. He is taken on many different kinds of lures and baits, but the Swedish pimple and the "airplane bait" are the two leaders.

Prime ice fishing lakes are Minnetonka, Mille Lacs, Leech, Winnibigoshish, Rainy, Kabetogama, and Vermilion. There are many other excellent fishing spots too numerous to list here.

Regarding licenses, Minnesota does charge extra for a "dark house" for spearing or ice fishing. This is in addition to the fishing license. Such a fish shanty must have the owner's name painted on the outside. It is unlawful for non-residents to spear any fish in Minnesota at any time; however, they may fish in a licensed shanty.

MISSOURI—Missouri Conservation Commission, Highway 50 West, Jefferson City

Because of its borderline climate, Missouri has good ice fishing only in cold winters and in restricted parts of the state. There are no special ice fishing rules. During severe winters, however, there is some fishing through the ice on Lake of the Ozarks, where fishermen are primarily after big crappies.

MONTANA—Department of Fish and Game, Helena

Trout head the list of important fish caught in the winter in the big state of Montana, where the most popular ice fishing spots are Georgetown Lake near Anaconda and Brown's Lake near Ovando. The Missouri River and impoundments between Townsend and Holter Dam are other hot spots. Montana uses the area system of fishing regulations, but the general restrictions statewide are rather liberal. Montana is very touchy about dumping live minnows, carp, or goldfish into its waters. All waters of the state are closed to the use of carp or goldfish for bait. Snagging of kokanee (sockeye) salmon is legal.

NEBRASKA—Game, Forestation and Parks Commission, State Capitol, Lincoln

The motto in "Nebraskaland" is "we do have some local restrictions but we attempt to make catching fish just as easy and as much fun as possible and avoid imposing a lot of unnecessary rules."

Many visiting anglers haul in a fair array of fish, but yellow perch, bluegills, Northern pike, largemouth bass, and crappie make up the bulk of the catch. They do most of this fish catching with minnows and various spoons and jigs. The state offers a neat folder entitled *Where to Fish in Nebraskaland*. Heavily fished winter waters are in the Valentine Waterfowl Refuge just south of Valentine. Another hot spot is Smith Lake south of Rushville.

NEVADA—State Fish and Game Commission, Box 678, Reno

Wildhorse and Wilson reservoirs in north central Nevada are the ice fishing hot spots for rainbow trout, the key winter fish here in a state where one would not normally think of ice fishing. Most of the winter angling is done with bait, canned shrimp, canned corn, and minnows.

NEW HAMPSHIRE—Fish and Game Department, 34 Bridge Street, Concord

Lake trout, shad (or Great Lakes whitefish), chain pickerel, yellow perch, and cusk are the most important fish for ice anglers in New Hampshire. Winnipesaukee, Squam, Winnisquam, and Newfound lakes are the most important for lake trout and shad in New Hampshire.

NEW JERSEY—Department of Fish and Game, 230 W. State Street, Trenton

New Jersey's ice fishing season lasts from January 1 to the middle of February. The eastern chain pickerel and yellow perch comprise the bulk of the winter catch, but other species, such as largemouth bass, catfish, and white perch, are also important in different waters.

NEW MEXICO—Department of Game and Fish, State Capitol, Santa Fe

Rainbow trout is the most popular winter fish in this state. Some ice fishing is done by only a few on some of the trout lakes, such as Bluewater Lake, and at times on El Vado, Storrie, and Maxwell lakes, when fish are available. These are reservoirs and sometimes are empty.

NEW YORK—Department of Conservation, Albany

Walleye, Northern pike, pickerel, perch, and smelt are the leading winter fish for New York ice anglers. In this state, live minnows and jigs with small spoons, perch eyes, and cut bait are the favorite terminal tackle.

Oneida Lake, Lake Champlain, the St. Lawrence River, and the bays along the south shore of Lake Ontario are the most productive New York ice fishing waters. It is illegal to take fish through the ice in trout waters, unless permitted by Department of Conservation orders.

NORTH DAKOTA—State Game and Fish Department, Bismarck

The undisputed number one fishing spot in North Dakota is the Garrison Reservoir, which includes the Garrison Tailrace (open water below the dam) and the Snake Creek Reservoir, an arm of the Garrison Reservoir. Other good winter fishing spots include Lake Ashtabula, Gravel Lake (for rainbow trout), Lake Metigoshe and Lake Darling. The State Game and Fish Department reported Lake Garrison was best for Northern pike, walleye, and perch; Garrison Dam Tailrace, pike, sauger, and walleye; Lake Ashtabula, perch; and Lakes Darling and Metigoshe, pike, perch, and walleyes. The general winter fishing season is January 1 through March 21.

North Dakota fishermen are said to be "dyed-in-the-wool" minnow fishermen. In recent years, however, they have been discovering that lures can be more productive at certain times. In the famous Garrison waters, where pike up to thirty pounds are often caught, a hot lure is the bucktail jig fished slowly on the bottom. Pike fishermen in this state are also using more dead smelt and finding it very good for pike. Check the laws carefully for lakes where minnows and other live baits are prohibited. In these waters anglers turn to salmon eggs, perch eyes, corn, marshmallows, and small wet flies and spoons.

OHIO—Division of Wildlife, Department of Natural Resources, 1500 Dublin Road, Columbus

Ohio is one of the big ice fishing states, with around a quarter of a million winter anglers who go primarily for bluegills, crappies, and perch. The best lakes for these panfish are Mogadore, Indian Lake, and Lake Erie.

Each tipup must have a waterproof tag giving the user's name and address. Ice fishing shanties and other fishing shelters on the ice in Lake Erie also must have the name and mailing address of the owner.

Generally across the state, Ohio's liberalized regulations provide for no closed seasons, no minimum size, and no creel or possession limits. The fishing license year begins March 1. Free lists of public fishing lakes and ponds with notes on facilities are available from the Natural Resources Department in Columbus.

OREGON—Game Commission, Portland

Some Oregon waters are open to year round fishing. Others are not. Summer creel limits apply to trout in this state, where only hook and line fishing is legal.

Worms and salmon eggs are the leading baits in Oregon. Officials of the Game Commission list Prineville Reservoir and Ochoco Reservoir as the best ice fishing waters.

PENNSYLVANIA—Fish Commission, Harrisburg

Ice fishing in Pennsylvania is really booming as a major wintertime fun activity, with nearly 100,000 fishermen taking part. The variety of fish is a big attraction here. The size and creel limits on bass, pickerel, muskies, panfish and Northern pike are the same as during the other seasons of the year.

In the northeast region, Lake Wallenpaupack, with 5,670 acres, near Hawley, Pennsylvania, is a hot spot for bass, walleye, pickerel, trout, panfish, and smelt. Because it is so large, it is a late freezer. In Pike County, White Deer Lake, Fairview Lake, and Greeley Lake are the top three. The northwest region boasts Presque Isle Bay in

Erie County as the most popular and heaviest fished. Perch and smelt with some Northern pike and large-mouth bass are the big attractions. Late in the season, bluegills and black crappie are the main fish. Vast 16,000-acre Pymatuning Lake in Crawford County is another favorite spot for ice fishing, with crappies and bluegills the most common fishes, although bass and walleye turn up often.

Stevenson Dam in Cameron County, Black Moshannon Lake in Centre County, and Beaver Lake in Lycoming County get special mention in the north central region of Pennsylvania. Across the southern band of counties, there are many excellent ice fishing lakes. Fish warden supervisors are your best sources of information on the local level for conditions, baits, and local fish-catching techniques.

Pennsylvania laws are very liberal. Fishing licenses from one year are good through February 28 of the new year.

RHODE ISLAND—Department of Agriculture and Conservation, Veterans Memorial Building, 83 Park Street, Providence

The nation's smallest state has a very respectable number of ice fishermen, around 30,000 out of the approximately 90,000 anglers who fish in warmer weather. These anglers fish through February 20 primarily for pickerel, yellow perch, and largemouth bass. On larger fish, they use golden shiners and mummichogs, or "mummies," for bait. To catch panfish, most popular rigs are jigging lines, small lures, and perch eyes or cut bait.

Rhode Island fishermen like Worden, Watchaug, Chapman, Pascoag, Watermans, Stump, and Flat River reservoirs for ice fishing. Trout of all species may be taken through the ice from December 1 through February 20, and there is no general size limit. Ice fishing, as in many other states, is restricted to daylight hours only. Check local restrictions carefully, because bait fish may not be used in some waters.

SOUTH DAKOTA—Department of Game, Fish and Parks, Pierre

South Dakota has exceptionally good ice fishing for large Northern pike and walleyes and only recently made pike spearing legal in the Missouri River reservoir area.

Also new and exciting is a developing ice fishing sport for rainbow and brown trout in the lakes in the Black Hills, where limits are liberal.

South Dakota's Missouri River reservoirs boast exceptional growth for pike. Two-year-old pike of six pounds and over are common. Walleyes of twelve pounds and up are also frequently taken by ice fishermen who use traditional methods—tipups and handlines.

Be prepared to drill through plenty of ice. This state gets more than its share of cold weather, but not tremendous amounts of snow. Ice four feet thick is not uncommon.

Best areas are the reservoirs for pike and the northeast lakes area for walleyes. Trout fishing in the winter is best in the Black Hills. South Dakota also has good winter angling for panfish.

UTAH—Fish and Game Department, 1596 W. North Temple, Salt Lake City

Utah has a unique through-the-ice Bonneville cisco

dipping sport, the only way you can take these tasty fish here. This dipping occurs at Bear Lake, when the ice covers the shallows. Dip netters chop through to work their nets. Utah Lake has a large carp seining operation the year round, even through the ice. The Bonneville cisco is a small, silvery fish which is very good to eat and not difficult to take with nets. It is a member of the whitefish family, and its nearest cousin is found in the Great Lakes region. Besides good eating, the Bonneville cisco makes an excellent bait fish and is sold for bait throughout Idaho, Utah, and Wyoming.

Dip netters work best in January and February, when the cisco spawn. Most commonly caught fish through the ice are rainbow trout and white bass. Rainbows come from Flaming Gorge Reservoir and Mantua Reservoir. White bass come out of Utah Lake.

VERMONT—Fish and Game Commission, Montpelier

Walleye, yellow perch, Northern pike, and smelt are the most important fish. Lake Champlain is the number one ice fishing water in Vermont. There is no general closed season on many other species, including bullheads, carp, bowfin, suckers, mullet, garfish, etc.

VIRGINIA—Game and Inland Fish Commission, Richmond

The Virginia Game and Inland Fisheries Commission legalized ice fishing in inland waters February 15, 1962. There is not a great deal of ice fishing in the state because of the marginal ice conditions.

However, largemouth, smallmouth, spotted, and striped bass, pickerel, walleye, Northern pike and muskies, and all the panfish are under a continuous open season statewide. See the fish law digest for local regulations.

WASHINGTON—Department of Game, 600 N. Capitol Way, Olympia

Perch and rainbow trout are the most important fish caught in the winter in Washington, which has county-by-county rules, seasons, and restrictions.

There are many excellent ice fishing spots in this lake-rich state. Worth mentioning are Hog Canyon Lake in the Tyler area, Williams Lake in southern Spokane County north of Colville, and Eloika Lake in Spokane County.

WEST VIRGINIA—Department of Natural Resources, Charleston

West Virginia is a borderline ice fishing state with winter angling limited to the few impoundments in higher elevations where they have extended periods of ice cover. Otherwise, West Virginia lakes and ponds do not freeze hard and long enough to contribute to major winter sport.

WISCONSIN—Conservation Department, Box 450, Madison

The yellow perch is the fish most often taken through the ice followed by the Northern pike, walleye, bluegill, crappie, and trout. Wisconsin ice fishermen favor the mayfly larvae, mousey, and goldenrod grub for bluegills, perch, and trout, and dead minnows bobbed slowly up and down for Northerns, walleyes, and crappie. Live minnows on tipups are also common.

Lakes Mendota and Winnebago are the leaders for winter perch fishing; the Mississippi River, Shawano Lake, and many others too numerous to mention are tops for pike, with walleyes and bluegills also found in great numbers in Winnebago and the Mississippi River. The Mississippi is tops for crappies. Big Green Lake is the best lake trout lake, and Devils Lake, Sauk County, is best for other trout fishing. Because of its widely scattered lakes and streams, Wisconsin has a long list of seasons and special restrictions which should be checked carefully.

WYOMING—Game and Fish Commission, Cheyenne

There is no special license. Ice fishermen favor Jackson Lake in Teton County, Buffalo Bill Reservoir in Park County, Flaming Gorge Reservoir in Sweetwater County, Lake Hattie in Albany County, and all of the North Platte River reservoirs.

The primary winter fish is different in each area. In some areas the mackinaw, rainbow, and brown trout are king. Ling is king in other areas and provides plenty of winter sport. Wyoming regulations are not much different from the other states. It is unlawful to use fish eggs, real or artificial, or corn as bait.

Wyoming's Game and Fish Commission produces a colorful road-map type of fishing brochure and a 42-page *Wyoming Fishing Guide* to help you pick the species, water, and season you like. It lists all the information a visiting winter fisherman could want.

CANADA

ALBERTA—Division of Lands and Forests, Terrance Building, Edmonton, Alberta

Lake whitefish, Northern pike, and perch are the three most important winter fish in Alberta, in that order. Popular lakes for ice fishing are Wabamun and Lac Ste. Ann, but there are many, many lakes with excellent fishing. There is no closed season or general size limit on grayling trout, Rocky Mountain whitefish, lake trout, pike, pickerel, and perch.

BRITISH COLUMBIA—Department of Recreation and Conservation, Fish and Game Branch, Victoria

There are no closed seasons for fishing in British Columbia, with a few local exceptions. Ice fishing rules are the same as for open water fishing. Anyone making an opening in the ice is required to guard it or mark it to prevent someone from falling in.

Rainbow, Eastern brook, kokanee, and char are the leading British Columbia fishes. They are caught mostly on bait such as worms, shrimp, and cut meat. Spinners and corn are also successfully used.

Kootenay, Okanagan, and Shuswap are the largest lakes used by ice fishermen here.

MANITOBA—Department of Mines and Natural Resources, Winnipeg

Most regulations that apply to summer angling also apply to ice fishing. Any shelter must be clearly identified on the outside with the name and address of the owner, and shelters must be removed from the ice no later than

March 31 each year. Most important winter fish are perch, walleyes, pike, and trout. Since perch are most abundant throughout the province, naturally more are caught. Rainbow trout are the champions of the larger winter species caught here. Native lake trout populations are also causing a big stir.

NEWFOUNDLAND—Department of Mines and Resources, St. Johns

One line is legal for ice fishing, although the angler may cut as many holes and move as often as need be. Speckled trout are the most important fish taken in the winter, and live worms lead the favorite bait parade.

NORTHWEST TERRITORIES—Department of Natural Resources, Ottawa

There are no specific ice fishing rules or regulations. The only sport fishing is for trout, grayling, and Arctic char—the three most important fish in the Northwest Territories.

There are literally thousands of productive lakes and rivers for winter fishing, with Great Slave and Great Bear lakes the largest and best known. Great Bear, by the way, is free of ice all the way across only about two months each year, from around late June to late August.

NOVA SCOTIA—Department of Trade and Industry, Halifax

With the exception of fishing for smelt, ice fishing is illegal in Nova Scotia. Smelt fishing is very popular with the natives, who take smelt in large numbers from the various rivers which regularly freeze over.

ONTARIO—Lands and Forests Department, Parliament Building, Toronto 2

Minnows are favored baits. There were more than 4,000 fish huts on Lake Simcoe alone by mid-February, 1965. Lake Nipissing and Lake Temagami in the North Bay district are very popular too. Lake Couchiching is another good spot.

Ice huts or shanties must be removed by the end of March. The owner's name must be on the shelter, a regulation found in just about every ice fishing rule book in the United States as well as Canada. Lake trout, whitefish, and lake herring are the main attractions at Lake Simcoe. Perch, walleye, and pike are leading fish in waters such as Lake St. Clair near Detroit, Bay of Quinte, Frenchman's Bay, Lake St. Francis, Ottawa River, and Lake Nipissing.

PRINCE EDWARD ISLAND—Department of Industry and Natural Resources, Charlottetown, P.E.I.

There is considerable ice fishing on the island for salt water species, particularly smelt. The island has no special provisions regarding sport ice fishing. It is unlawful to jig for fish or use torches or other artificial light in catching salmon or trout.

QUEBEC—Province de Quebec, Hotel du gouvernement, Quebec

There are no special ice fishing rules in Quebec. Simply obey the regular angling laws and limits, and you are set the year round here. Quebec has developed an elaborate tourist-attracting network of ice fishing festivals with prizes and all the trimmings to encourage winter tourists in this vacationland.

Prized fish here are the glamour species—speckled, brown, rainbow, and lake trout. Some areas boast land-locked salmon. Yellow perch, walleyes, and Northern pike are caught throughout the winter here, where they are vicious feeders. The ice fishing season is a long one, from around Christmas to April.

Main centers of winter fishing in the Montreal district are the northwest sector of Missisquoi Bay, and the bays of Carillon and of Rigaud. Yellow perch are the big fish in this area. Pike and walleye are also taken.

YUKON TERRITORY—Department of Fisheries, P.O. Box 2410, Whitehorse, Y.T.

Ice fishing is not very common in the Yukon Territory, but it is available in great quantities for those who want it. There are no closed seasons for sport fishing, and the daily limit is generous.

Non-residents must pay two dollars for a fishing license: Of all the fish available, lake trout, whitefish, and pike are the big three here. Prime lakes: Teslin Lake, Lake La-Berge, Kluane Lake, and Marsh Lake. There is no spear-ing allowed. Live fish or fish eggs are prohibited in the territory.